Library 2020

Today's Leading Visionaries Describe Tomorrow's Library

Edited by Joseph Janes

THE SCARECROW PRESS, INC.
Lanham • Toronto • Plymouth, UK
2013

Published by Scarecrow Press, Inc.
A wholly owned subsidiary of The Rowman & Littlefield Publishing Group, Inc.
4501 Forbes Boulevard, Suite 200, Lanham, Maryland 20706
http://www.scarecrowpress.com

Estover Road, Plymouth PL6 7PY, United Kingdom

British Library Cataloguing in Publication Information Available

Library of Congress Cataloging-in-Publication Data

Library 2020 : today's leading visionaries describe tomorrow's library / edited by Joseph Janes. pages
cm
Includes bibliographical references.
ISBN 978-0-8108-8714-5 (pbk. : alk. paper) -- ISBN 978-0-8108-8715-2 (ebook) 1. Library science-
-Forecasting. 2. Libraries--Forecasting. 3. Libraries--Aims and objectives. 4. Libraries--Information
technology. 5. Libraries and the Internet. 6. Libraries and society. I. Janes, Joseph, editor of compila-
tion.
Z665.L587 2013
020--dc23
2013009872

™
◉   The paper used in this publication meets the minimum requirements of American
National Standard for Information Sciences Permanence of Paper for Printed Library
Materials, ANSI/NISO Z39.48-1992.

Printed in the United States of America

Contents

Introduction

Joseph Janes

Welcome to 2020. We know a few things about this year; there will almost certainly be a presidential election, heaven help us, which means the campaigning should start about the time this book is published. There will also be an Olympic Games, a leap year, and, if Wikipedia is to be believed, the Giant Magellan Telescope will be completed, the Russian Space Agency will be mining helium from the moon, and the California High-Speed Rail system will be finished. Whether Wikipedia will still be around, they don't say.

Why 2020 for a book of future visions of libraries? Why not? It's far enough out that some exciting things might well have happened but not so far out as to have to resort to shiny-jump suit and hovercar predictions left over from 1965 about 2000. It seemed a goodly amount of lead time for an esteemed and varied group of thinkers and doers and dreamers and screamers to ponder futures of all sorts.

And that's precisely what we have here. I solicited participation from a variety of folks, mostly friends as well as some people I admire a great deal, and asked them to fill in the blank: "The library in 2020 will be _____." Here's the rest of what I asked:

> You can go on from there. You could discuss a specific library (one you work in, use, know, etc., or not), a kind of library, libraries in general, the way professionals or clientele think about them, or something even more interesting. Be bold, be inspirational, be hopeful, be true, be provocative, be realistic, be depressing, be light-hearted, be thoughtful, be fun . . . be yourself, and for heaven's sake, don't be boring!
>
> What I have in mind is a collection of short pieces—between 1,500 and 2,500 words, maybe 4–7 pages each, from a wide range of voices from within the library field and beyond, which I hope will add richness and texture to the discussion and bring perspectives we don't always hear.

Mission accomplished, in spades. What you will find here runs the gamut on lots of dimensions, utopias to dystopias, specifics to broad overviews, touching on a large number of issues, settings, challenges, successes, and potential pitfalls. Some of these will make you happy, some will make you mad, a few might depress you, and all of them, in one way or another, has the potential to make you think, or rethink, or question, or imagine what might be, which is exactly what I had in mind.

Once they started to come in, I realized that my work was just beginning, since there's no obvious order in which to present these; in reading through them, though, I began to see patterns—you will likely, of course, see others—that echo ideas I've had for many years about the nature of libraries and what they do and are. Hence, you find here very broad groupings about "stuff," "people," "community," "place," and "leadership and vision." I've long maintained that these are the essential and basic building blocks of libraries, and lo and behold, here they are again. I hope none of my contributors minds the environs I've situated them in, and if the neighbors play their music too loud, just let me know. And yet, within those categories, there's tremendous variety and individuality; bear in mind while reading, though, that those groupings are entirely mine.

And then, naturally, I get the last word. Or, more correctly, the chance to spin a few ideas of my own. I didn't try to summarize or comment on anybody else's work; I don't know any better than anybody else, though I do think I have a few notions to offer for your consideration.

In a sense, you could think of these as messages in a bottle, sent forward into an uncertain future that we are all part of creating every day. Writing a book about the future is a fool's errand, of course; if you're right, then it was all too obvious, and if you're wrong, well, then, ha ha ha on you. Lots of people also say they'd rather create the future than predict it, which I support entirely, and as you'll notice, many of the people you hear from here are doing precisely that. It's nonetheless worthwhile, particularly at moments when it all seems up in the air, to take a step or two back and fix your eyes on the horizon and see what you see. Nobody knows how much of the following will, or even should, come true, but I'm optimistic enough to believe that when we get to 2020—sooner than some of us might like to think—more people will be pondering where libraries go from there, and on and on.

Of course, I want to express my gratitude to everybody who took the time and energy to spin these futures and share them with the wider world. I very much appreciate your participation, and I owe you all a drink. Special thanks go to my tireless and always-supportive publisher, Charles Harmon, who, once again nudged and prodded me most elegantly and gently toward bringing this to fruition. And, as ever, to my beloved husband Terry, who makes everything in my life much more interesting.

I

Stuff

Chapter One

The Annoyed Librarian

The library in 2020 will be just like the library today, except without all the books, music, and movies.

The books will be the first to go, because they're already going. E-books are becoming more popular every year, and Amazon announced recently that it's selling more e-books than print books. That trend is only going to continue because everyone likes e-books. Readers like them for the convenience, Amazon likes them because they don't take up warehouse space, and publishers like them because they can keep e-books out of libraries. Publishers really don't like libraries, which is why the few publishers willing to license e-books to libraries give such bad deals on them—not that it prevents libraries from throwing good money after bad to get their relative handful of e-books into library patrons' hands.

But wait, you protest, libraries will still be able to supply print books! Not for long, they won't. Eventually, print books will go away, at least for the most part. The big exception will be children's books, which will probably be around for quite a while longer. Spilling soda on a paperback book is much less of a problem than spilling it on an iPad. Plus, children like the tactile sensation of print books, and a generation of children will grow up dissatisfied that they can no longer enjoy the feeling of a new print book for readers over ten years old. There will also still be small publishers putting out specialized books or fiction for niche markets. But the thing about books for specialized or niche markets is that not many people want to read them, and the mantra for most public libraries is that unless books are popular, libraries don't want them. The major publishers will slowly move away from print books as they figure out how to make money and survive in a digital world. Or they won't figure out a way to survive, and the only new books available will be Internet fan fiction. Either way, no more print books for adults in libraries. This might not happen by 2020, but it'll happen within the lifetime of most people reading this. The best-case scenario for getting books is that libraries invest in lots of e-book readers, buy books for them, and then lend out the readers. If you've ever seen the underside of the average library DVD after a few loans, you can imagine how well those Nooks and Kindles will hold up.

Speaking of library DVDs, there won't be any of those either. By 2020, DVDs will be about as popular as VHS tapes. New movies won't even be released on a physical medium. The only way you'll be able to purchase a movie will be digitally. Netflix knows this, which is why they split their DVD service from their streaming video service. It's really going to be annoying for everyone, especially libraries. Have you tried purchasing a digital movie? On Amazon, for example, you can buy digital songs or albums and download them free of DRM (digital rights management), but if you buy a digital movie from them, you can only watch it in your browser or a dedicated application. Forget about lending it to a friend to watch because that's going to be impossible unless you give them your password to whatever service you got the movie from. For libraries, it means the end of providing popular videos at all. While there are some specialized video-streaming services available to libraries, public libraries are unlikely to invest heavily in things like the Boring Documentary Archive. That's what academic libraries are for. The masses who want to get their latest superhero flick from the library will be out of luck.

And music, long a staple at public libraries? You can probably tell where I'm going with this one. That'll be going away to because sales of music attached to a physical medium are just about over. The CD is going the way of the eight-track tape. By 2020, it'll be easier to buy music on vinyl than CD, and the popular music that libraries want to provide will all be available cheaply and digitally, just like it is now. For the price of a half-dozen CDs in the bad old days, people can buy one hundred songs they like from iTunes and never even have to listen to the tedious filler tracks between the hit songs. Add in services like Spotify, and it's obvious that music is cheaper and more accessible than ever before—except at libraries. Sure, there is some digital music available through libraries, but the selection's not great and not likely to improve. When music is available in a physical medium, music publishers can't stop libraries from buying that medium and lending it out. But music publishers have no more incentive to allow lots of music to stream affordably to library patrons than book publishers have to provide e-books to libraries. Music publishers are the most aggressive and ruthless publishers around, and they probably don't like libraries either. Libraries could start buying iPods and lending them out, but that would be ridiculous. People aren't going to visit a library to borrow an iPod just to hear a hit song.

There will still be some fun things available at the library, like video games. A lot of video games are migrating to controlled online networks, but as long as video-game consoles exist, libraries can still buy them. They can still lure the kiddies into the library and have them Wiiing and Xboxing for hours. They can even still do this under the false pretense that they're trying to lure the kiddies with the video games, hoping they'll stay for the books, at least if the kiddies are young enough to still enjoy the print children's books available.

And of course, there will still be computers. Hulking old desktop PCs with small monitors are dirt cheap these days, and libraries will easily be able to fill the space left by the dwindling book collection with more banks of computers. That way the poor who can't afford even a low-end computer or an Internet connection will still be able to hunt for jobs, find out about the exciting events of the day, or surf for porn. Libraries will be able to have so many computers they can get rid of the annoying lines and waitlists. This would be no small accomplishment. Those of us with a computer—desktop, laptop, tablet, smartphone, or all four—always ready to turn on and tune in can't really understand what life is like for people who need a computer for some life-saving activity like applying for a job and have to wait in line behind some teenagers fooling around on MySpace. Libraries will do a better job of bridging the digital divide when people can just wander in anytime and use a computer.

And with those computers, there will still be lots of subscription databases for people to do some sort of reading and research. Schoolchildren can still look up articles on whatever it is schoolchildren research these days. The old guys haunting the newspaper racks will become the old guys haunting online news services. People can get their social media fixes. Budding writers can read their way through Project Gutenberg and create new literature.

Except for children's books and online databases, libraries will evolve even further from books and media than they're already doing. They will become much more like community centers than most libraries are now. They might add food banks and postal services, like some libraries are already doing, but the main emphasis will still be on cultural products. With the commercial books, music, and movies gone, libraries will focus more on local creation. This might take the shape of so-called makerspaces or writers writing at library computers, but it's just as likely to focus on local achievements that are exhibited in or loaned through libraries as created there. Unknown writers and local artists will display works and give talks and workshops.

There will be a lot more talks and workshops about everything, as the custodians of culture formerly known as librarians work harder to bring people together for something besides books. Arts and crafts, computers, life skills, instead of competing with local bookstores, libraries will start competing with the more practical offerings of local community colleges. Out of sheer necessity, public libraries will be more engaged in active education than passive education for the first time in their history.

Children will still come to hang out in a safe place after school. The homeless will still find warm seats and restrooms. People will still come to use the computers and read the news. Meeting rooms will be full and any classrooms busy. There will still be socializing and discussion. The library won't be a bad place at all. In fact, it will still be a good place, of central importance for the community. It just won't quite be a library anymore.

The Annoyed Librarian is possibly the most successful, respected, and desirable librarian of her generation. She has no other interest than to bring her wit and wisdom to the huddled librarian masses yearning to breathe free. The Annoyed Librarian is a free spirit, and you are lucky to have her.

Chapter Two

Kristin Fontichiaro

These are the facts. The old library was passive, asleep, an arsenal in time of peace; the librarian a sentinel before the doors. . . . The new library is active, an aggressive, educating force in the community . . . an army in the field with all guns limbered; and the librarian occupies a field of active usefulness second to none.
—Melvil Dewey, 1888

The library of 2020 is just one exit past today's five-year plan, and yet, it is a road under construction. How quickly we've seen our world change from the start of one long-range plan to the next! Materials are changing so radically, and it's easier than ever for people to access stuff without us. When free Kindle books or Nook downloads outprice the cost of a bus ticket or the car fuel for a library visit, or when it is faster to search online than to ask the librarian, then library-as-collection is a dangerous basket in which to put too many of our eggs. When books are freely or near-freely available elsewhere, being "the book place" is a dangerous stance to defend. *Libraries can no longer count on describing themselves as the repositories for stuff.*

Against the backdrop of continuing national economic downturn, politicians have scrutinized every expense. How much does a pothole cost? How many library books is that worth? Do we keep an extra firefighter or outreach coordinator? School nurse or teacher librarian? Services become commodities, each priced and laid out like a rummage sale's dollar-a-bag event: school boards, university regents, and town councils know there's only so much money, and so few things fit in their bags. *"The public good" is no longer a sufficient rationale for libraries.*

In the wake of the 2012 presidential election, in which the themes were simplified into "we built it" against "big government," the divide between Americans widened. While it is obvious that libraries *are* filling a gap, primarily in terms of digital access, what motivates a twenty-year-old to support libraries when she doesn't need storytime or large-print materials? How does one convince the self-made entrepreneur with a household full of mobile devices that he should pay to populate someone else's device with content? The libraries-for-the-weak narrative is politically tenuous and uncertain. *Libraries can no longer portray themselves as supporters of the underserved— their narrative must include everyone.*

To thrive in 2020, libraries need to make a ferocious and sustained shift in focus from collection to users. The culture of makerspaces gives us a fresh vision of what is possible for libraries. A makerspace is both a facility and an organization in which people of like interests come together to individually or collectively create works with shared tools and space. While the term *makerspace* is often most affiliated with wood carpentry, metal work, electrical work, or robotics, it is becoming an umbrella term for any space and organizing group centered on making things. Makerspaces, quilt guilds, fab labs, potters' studios, and hackerspaces are all closely aligned in mission: to support people who want to share experiences in making things. Dale Grover of Maker Works in Ann Arbor, Michigan, describes a makerspace as "tools plus support plus community." It's a great metaphor we can borrow to envision thriving libraries in 2020.

Adopting a makerspace culture diversifies libraries' long-outdated role as shushing book distributors. It redefines the library as a place of creation, not consumption, and it appeals across socioeconomic and geographical divides. And by doing so, it promotes entrepreneurship to jumpstart much-needed economic growth. In this chapter, we will look at makerspaces and draw parallels to libraries' potential future.

TOOLS

A makerspace begins with tools. Either via membership fees or member contributions to a cooperative, a makerspace acquires high-cost shop, construction, and creation machines that a single owner could neither afford nor find room to store. From laser cutters to embroidery machines, computerized lathes to 3-D printers, makerspaces are spaces with tools that make visions come to life. Makers, the often-amateur creators and inventors who belong to the group, have access to all of the tools and space in which to work.

Libraries are historical tool sharers. Our tools are the books, recordings, videos, toys, puzzles, musical instruments, garden implements, cake pans, and other items that entrepreneurial librarians have collected for circulation over the years. Our tools also include in-house equipment: computer labs and individual terminals, flannel boards, puppet stages, copy machines, microfiche readers, study rooms, large work tables, and fireside chairs. These concrete or virtual objects are not an end; they are a *means to an end*, the seeds that lead to later fruit. A picture book is a raw material out of which a bedtime dramatization will occur. A cookbook (or a cake pan!) is an essential tool for learning a new cuisine. *Consumer Reports* is a resource for making a car purchase, and an academic journal is a tool for both earning tenure and sharing information. All of these are designed and selected because they are tools for a user's information journey. It should be said that although we pay up-front for library resources, they do not really gain community value until they are *used*. An unused resource is a useless tool, and thoughtful, locally driven collection development helps us do a better job of buying better equipment. It is our job to buy resources that our community uses.

In libraries, we're *good* at tools. However, digitization and the shift from doctrine of first sale to a licensing model challenge this core role of libraries. We must transition into being providers of *experiences*, not just stuff.

SUPPORT

Beyond access to equipment, one of the appeals for participating in a maker-space is the support that accompanies the membership. Imagine that you want to make a custom chess set. You have your makerspace membership, which gives you access to a laser cutter or a 3-D printer. Which do you want to use? And how do you use it? A makerspace's formal and informal support networks are there to help.

Perhaps you will start with formal instruction in which you will learn, hands-on, how to use the equipment. In the case of 3-D printing, perhaps you'll learn how to mock up your object in the software and then learn to thread the reel of meltable plastic into the machine itself so that it prints properly. Maybe you'll take a project-based approach, in which you will learn the tool in the context of creating a simple starter project: a 3-D-printed key chain or a laser-cut sign.

Additionally, support comes from fellow makers. A novice at 3-D printing might get a just-in-time peer coaching from a more experienced user. Two experienced users might swap techniques. One maker might help another load something into a vehicle. Additionally, many makerspaces have support staff members who are skilled in using or fixing the machines. In-house repair expertise offers a maker an important benefit: more expedient use of time and money. If something breaks, a maker doesn't have to stop working for two weeks and learn to repair that computer-driven lathe or 3-D printer. Facility staff take the lead in troubleshooting or improving the machine's performance.

Let's port this concept into the library space. Libraries have long seen themselves as learning spaces for children. Information-literacy instruction has been another key area of support, teaching students and patrons how to unlock powerful knowledge that promotes lifelong learning in a way that, implemented well, moves them far beyond how to navigate the library and its collections. Another is classes or one-on-one tutorials on digital literacy skills: from office software to social media to video production. In some cases, libraries loan meeting space to community organizations that provide support, from bike-safety events to tax-prep sessions.

A true commitment to support as a key library function means coming to terms with librarianship as a *service profession*. The word *service* is fraught with negative connotations, conjuring up visions of *Upstairs, Downstairs* or, worse, being on "permahold" with an automated phone system. For our patrons to believe that we are there to support them—as *specific individuals*, not some abstract group like "the town"—we must reaffirm our commitment to supporting and helping others as they go about learning, creating, and improving for work or pleasure.

Here, we need to take a deep and uncomfortable look at our frontline library representatives. Have you ever mailed in a check to cover an overdue fine or put a book back so you could avoid the circulation desk when you discovered self-checkout was broken? I visit a lot of libraries to refresh the library courses I teach, and I admit that I have done both. These aren't tool problems: they are people problems that hold us back from achieving our full potential in the community. Somewhere along the line, we've convinced ourselves that we have more important things to worry about than how we treat patrons. If we want to be perceived as a Nordstrom-quality experience in our communities and funded accordingly, then we have to turn on the Nordstrom-quality demeanor and *welcome* patrons into what is, in truth, *their* library. We are stewards of *their* collection and facility. Marketing can't change face-to-face stings. Libraries are in the business of people, not stuff, and they need excellent frontline service who live that belief.

When patrons encounter enthusiastic service and support, it is a paradigm shift. Consider the childhood librarian who held books behind the desk just for you, the circulation-desk clerk who cuts you some slack when you forgot to return your books during a family emergency, the surge protectors that proliferated in libraries with electricity during Hurricane Sandy–struck communities, the sign welcoming beverages in the stacks, the links to tax forms or polling stations. It was those moments of support—not the physical objects we checked out—that added value to our lives. Those are the human touches that resonate and make us love our physical and virtual libraries and librarians, making us eager to return and to continue funding them.

COMMUNITY

When you have been waiting all afternoon for your 3-D-printed masterpiece to finish, or you've tied your last quilting knot, or your robot finally—finally!—walks backward, you want to be able to turn to someone who will think it's as cool as you do. Therefore, the third aspect of makerspace culture is community: the sense that we are on a common journey. Makers enjoy makerspaces and hackers enjoy hackerspaces and quilters enjoy quilting bees not only because they are engaging in their hobby but also because they enjoy being with people like them. Some makerspaces hold special-member open houses, cookouts, or celebrations. They come together at maker festivals, art fairs, quilt festivals, or hackathons to practice their craft, talk shop, swap tips, tackle a bigger-than-the-individual project. A sense of trust and collegiality develops, along with the collective urge to raise the bar and keep doing better work.

As families continue to disperse in response to economic shifts and a globalized economy, and as the fervor over social media applications like Facebook seem to be silently but consistently waning, I predict that American individuals will have a new hunger to come together for face-to-face interactions—and libraries are one of the last remaining noncommercial settings where this can happen. While their grandparents may have come together at church or a Rotary meeting, the patrons of 2020 may come together over personal interests (such as creating a robot) or over hobbies they can leverage into a civic domain (such as a hackathon to create a new app to manage municipal information or a millage campaign). The very high-speed, high-tech life that made the iPad and e-books possible is also creating a society that is disconnected from the things it creates, and there is a resurgence in learning the crafts and hobbies of the past: canning, sewing, woodworking, even the physical. Writers seek writing groups; musicians may seek a group of critical friends to offer rehearsal feedback. Whether or not the library intentionally positions itself to become the community center of the future is very much reliant on the librarians and library staff on the front lines.

We have a historic head start: storytime started as an event to build early-literacy community with preschool children. Over time, many libraries have expanded their storytime format in order to welcome parents as equal participants. As the children grow up together, so do the families. Keeping these rituals going so that the library remains a destination, not a grab-and-go quick errand, is the challenge for 2020. Web analysts talk about "sticky" experiences online: those experiences that keep visitors actively engaged on the site. Storytime is sticky. Summer reading events are sticky. We play host to a variety of civic and community groups, from knitting circles to scouting groups, which themselves are formed around communal purpose and social engagement. They are sticky.

How do we make libraries sticky for other patrons, like the twenty-something hipster mentioned earlier? What kinds of events lure those who can afford to buy e-books back into our spaces? How do we make libraries sticky for busy, stressed employees who can't make daytime events like book clubs or lunchtime concerts? For blue-collar workers who don't read for pleasure? For new immigrants? Empty-nesters? Career-changers? Entrepreneurs? Those are the challenges that great librarians are already considering that will linger long after 2020.

CONCLUSION

In this short space, we've drawn parallels between the growing popularity of makerspace culture and the metaphorical potential it holds for rethinking libraries in the post–e-book era.

Am I advocating that libraries become woodshop spaces, buzzing with drill presses and lathes, slathered in sawdust? No. Well, not for now, anyway (some architects are already noodling about the current trend of converting enormous retail spaces into libraries, where there is adequate square footage). Most current library facilities lack the space, ventilation, liability insurance, or industrial-grade electrical wiring to bring power tools into their space. For most libraries, this simply isn't practical or financially feasible.

But should libraries continue the decades-long transformation from being places that host stuff to places that host experiences? Absolutely. We have had knitting clubs and sewing groups in our libraries for some time now without being accused that such social hobbies are taking down the library-as-institution. If we allow knitting needles into our libraries, surely we want to extend similar privileges for all hobbyists so we do not accidentally create library programming that merely mirrors our own interests. Many libraries are looking into becoming *actual* small-scale makerspaces, purchasing 3-D printers for drop-in use and holding workshops on using 3-D microcontrollers. These activities have a small footprint that brings new partners and new patrons into the library. They are valuable, low-cost additions to a library's budget. For example, an Arduino microcontroller costs around $25, and a Raspberry Pi microcomputer costs around $35, very close to the price of a single library book! Who needs to feel an ownership in our physical space so they vote yes for the next millage? Who is our untapped community?

But it's more than makerspace *stuff*. It's about ambiance. A makerspace *culture* has the potential to do much more by inspiring libraries to envision themselves as places where all citizens feel welcome bringing their individual visions of creating and sharing. When librarians embrace each patron as a creator of his or her own future and themselves as partners in that future, an incredible synchronicity is ignited.

I can't wait for 2020.

Kristin Fontichiaro teaches at the University of Michigan. A member of the inaugural class of the American Library Association's Emerging Leaders program, she was named a Library Journal *"Mover and Shaker" in 2012. She blogs at http://fontichiaro.com/activelearning.*

BIBLIOGRAPHY

Dewey, Melvil. "Libraries as Related to the Educational Work of the State." Speech read before the Convocation of the University of the State of New York. July 1, 1888. Retrieved September 2, 2012, from http://books.google.com/books/about/Libraries_as_ related_to_the_educational.html?id=xmIEAAAAMAAJ.

Chapter Three

Elisabeth A. Jones

The library in 2020 will have been transformed by large-scale book digitization—for better or for worse. The extent and shape of this transformation will vary widely; a small-town public library will experience considerably different changes from those at a major research library, and the impact on the myriad forms of special library (corporate libraries, special collections, etc.) will vary as much as the libraries themselves. And to the extent that policies related to digital-information access shift—especially copyright law—so too will these transformations. This chapter will explore some of the ways in which increasingly commonplace digital access to books, as provided by entities like Google Books, the Internet Archive, and HathiTrust, might affect library structures and operations. It will also briefly suggest a few ways in which modifying current copyright law might improve the outlook. However, before delving into this exploration, a bit more context will be helpful. What do we mean by large-scale digitization initiatives? And what is the status of these projects now?

For the purposes of this chapter, the term *large-scale digitization initiative* or *LSDI* refers to projects where the goal is to scan and make searchable as many books as possible, at a relatively rapid pace, generally through partnerships between libraries and organizations like Google and the Internet Archive. Starting with the announcement of the Google Books Library Project (GBLP) in 2004 and the Internet Archive–based Open Content Alliance in 2005, the scale and speed of digitization increased by at least an order of magnitude over previous efforts (Howard; Internet Archive; St. Clair; Library of Congress; Project Gutenberg). In the last eight years, Google alone has scanned more than twenty million books, and the Internet Archive has scanned and/or integrated a few million also (Howard; Internet Archive).[1] While the IA has focused mainly on scanning public domain works, Google has also included in-copyright works from some libraries and has faced much-publicized legal challenges because of that (see Band; Samuelson; New York Law School).[2] These ongoing legal issues seem to have dimmed Google's enthusiasm for the project, and it has significantly scaled back its scanning within the last year (Howard). More recently, however, two additional LSDIs have emerged: HathiTrust and the Digital Public Library of America (DPLA). HathiTrust is a collaboration among 65 major research libraries, with the goal of preserving access to digital books—including those digitized by Google and the Internet Archive—over the long term and currently contains more than 10.5 million books (HathiTrust Digital Library; Wilkin 2). The DPLA remains amorphous at present; it is unclear whether it will ultimately go beyond the level of discussions and, if it does, what shape it will actually take (Carr). However, it has piqued widespread interest among both library leadership and funding agencies and has the potential to offer an alternate avenue for public access to digital books (Digital Public Library of America; Carr).

So, if this is where we are now, where does that leave us in 2020? Having been involved with these projects in some form for the past eight years,[3] I feel like I have at least some basis for forecasting some aspects of the next seven. And although it would be easy to lapse into cynicism regarding a phenomenon so heavily influenced by copyright and contract law, I choose to present an optimistic scenario for these predictions. So here goes. Google will have entirely stopped scanning with libraries by 2016, having scanned perhaps 10 million more books. When it stops scanning, it will keep the Google Books site up mainly to serve its publisher partnerships[4] and will ease some of the restrictions placed on books scanned from libraries under the initial contracts, in much the same way Microsoft did when it shut down Live Search Books (Nadella). For public domain works, this means that, among other things, the OCR will become part of the free PDF download (making those PDFs full-text searchable offline), and bulk downloading will be allowed, if not from Google itself, then through its library partners or other sites.[5] The Internet Archive will still be scanning, and supporting scanning at other institutions, but still at much the same (slower) rate that it is now. My crystal ball is unclear as to whether there will be a more modern and user-friendly central access point for those scans than the current IA site (http://archive.org/texts)—but I hope so. HathiTrust will continue to grow— and if it keeps going at its current rate, it will have at least 14 million books in its corpus (probably more). It will be able to offer full-text downloads of public-domain works to anyone, regardless of institutional affiliation, due to the relaxation of Google's restrictions, and will also allow bulk downloading and other big-data-style entry points into its corpus. It will also have addressed many of the major metadata issues that have been raised regarding

Google's book site (e.g., Duguid). And other digitization work will have sprung up as well—perhaps through the DPLA, perhaps elsewhere.

Because of all this work, books published before 1923, which are estimated to make up roughly 15–20 percent of the system-wide physical book collection (Lavoie and Dempsey; Wilkin), will be reasonably close to completely digitized—say, 90 percent. Free of copyright and most contractual restrictions, all of these books will be redundantly available through many services and on many devices, as well as print-on-demand. This will be the most significant contribution of LSDIs (at least, given current laws). For books that are in-print and in-copyright, only the technologies will have changed (i.e., there will be new e-readers, new formats, new modes of purchase and use); libraries will still need to purchase or license digital versions of these works, to the extent that publishers are willing to provide libraries with those options (see Shank). And then there are the works that fall between these two categories: namely, works that are still in copyright but out of print and works of indeterminate copyright status and/or ownership—so-called orphan works. However, let's set the last two categories of books (in-print/in-copyright and out-of-print/orphan) aside for the moment and explore some of the new opportunities for and threats to different kinds of libraries in an environment where virtually all public domain books are openly available in digital form.

These opportunities and threats will, I suggest, fall roughly along six axes: (1) changing the calculus of preservation vs. access, (2) increasing impetus for collaboration, (3) reimagining library spaces, (4) disintermediation between reader and resource, (5) continuing—or even magnifying—the need for guidance and instruction, and (6) increasing expectations of digital universality. The remainder of this piece will take a brief look at each of these axes in turn.

PRESERVATION AND ACCESS

Essentially, comprehensive digital access to very old works will radically alter the preservation/access calculus—indeed, even without comprehensiveness, this change has already begun. One of the key promises of digitization for libraries is that it allows for simultaneous preservation (of the physical) and access (to the digital). As the digital copy becomes the privileged one for use, the physical version can be held back in all but those rare circumstances in which the actual artifact is needed. Additionally, because the digital avatar will appear in search engines and other public-information contexts, it should increase the use of the information it contains without imperiling the physical artifact (and to the extent that the digital version is traceable to the collection from which it was scanned, will also provide publicity for that collection).

This will be especially transformative for major research libraries and special collections, who tend to serve as the custodians of large quantities of rare and/or fragile materials.[6]

However, the preservation/access picture is not entirely rosy. As digital access becomes more ubiquitous and stable, both public and academic libraries will undoubtedly face the temptation to deaccession physical copies of digitized works (see Rieger 29). And yet, the question of how to preserve the digital surrogates themselves is far from conclusively answered. As Oya Rieger notes in her masterful examination of these issues, "Numerous factors put digital data at risk. Many technologies disappear as product lines are replaced, and backward compatibility is not always guaranteed." The vulnerable infrastructure, she goes on, includes storage media, file formats and compression schemes, and dependencies on applications, Internet protocols, and standards (Rieger 24). Thus, before libraries take steps like deaccessioning public-domain print collections, serious thought will need to be given to the stability and sustainability of the digital corpus.

INTER-LIBRARY COLLABORATION

Especially for libraries with collections of significant size and/or uniqueness, increased opportunities for collaboration will abound, some of which will look more like obligations. Some such pooling of digital resources and expertise has already begun, in projects like HathiTrust and DPLA. However, over time, as the digital book corpus becomes more stable and useful, it will become strategically advantageous for libraries to consider working together to create shared print repositories for the works contained in that corpus, like those already established for journals provided through JSTOR ("JSTOR Establishes Paper Repositories"). As many have suggested, such collaboration would help to free up valuable library space and would reduce system-wide preservation costs because there would be fewer volumes to preserve and those volumes would see less use (see Sandler 17; Rieger 38–39; Courant). This would be one form of insurance for the long-term future, should many libraries decide to get rid of their copies of works that are freely available online. After all, today's digital books will likely still be viable in eight years—but what about in 80? Or 800? We know that print can last that long; though not every library need keep every book, some level of redundant, collaborative archiving will be essential to ensuring continued access to digitized works.

REIMAGINING LIBRARY SPACE

The reimagining of library space, to focus less on housing books and more on amenities and service for patrons, is already well underway now. But by 2020, the opportunities for such shifts will have increased a great deal. As already noted, access to digital versions of public-domain works will likely lead some libraries to deaccession those works and others to contribute their copies to collaborative print archives. Beyond this, however, research libraries in particular will have greater flexibility to move collections into off-site, high-density storage facilities, which are simultaneously better for preservation objectives, due to better climate control and less public manhandling (Rieger 30–31), and lower in cost than traditional open shelving (Courant and Nielsen). And since the books so shifted will have full-text searchable versions online (and since a certain amount of search is already possible even for works still in copyright), patrons will be able to better ascertain which offsite items they might actually need. Though this may cause a bit of an identity crisis for some libraries—what are we if we are not the place where one goes to find books?—it is a crisis worth pushing past. Libraries can be so much more—and reducing the existing spatial emphasis on book stacks can help to open our minds to the possibilities.

DISINTERMEDIATION

In a world of physical books, those books have to be physically retrieved from libraries. Patrons must interact with the library, at least cursorily, in order to obtain what they want to read. If essentially all of the public domain is freely available redundantly across the Web, there will be no need to interact with a library at all in order to procure these works. Indeed, to a great extent, this is already the case. This causes a great deal of anxiety in the library community, especially among libraries that depend on public (i.e., tax) support in order to stay open. If our patrons come to believe that everything is available without a library, what will be our role? To that anxiety, I have two reactions. First, consider the mission of the public library—the one nearest to me, for example, claims it strives "to promote the development of literate and informed citizens through open and equal access to cultural, intellectual, recreational, and information resources" (Ann Arbor District Library)—and then consider whether the vastly increased access to books LSDIs provide might actually serve that mission, despite the removal of library mediation from the information transactions involved. If it does, it begs the question: which is more important, the perpetuation of the library itself or the fulfillment of its mission? And second, I sincerely doubt that the library will be rendered so completely obsolete by 2020 in any case. For one thing, libraries are still a key provider of Internet access for millions of Americans (Becker, et al. 9), and without access to the Internet, online books may as well not exist at all. And although it may not be as visible, libraries will still have many roles to play in making digital materials findable, interoperable, and so on; the challenge will be to demonstrate the value of those roles to a public who still thinks of the library as little more than a free book store.

GUIDANCE AND INSTRUCTION

As a further corollary to the issue of disintermediation, I would suggest that librarians will still have a strong role to play in guidance and instruction—perhaps an even stronger one than they already play. A core commonality among all LSDIs to date is the utter absence of any kind of service layer. Assuming this remains true, to whom will their users turn when they hit a roadblock in their information-seeking process? From my own experiences working at the University of Michigan's Graduate Library reference desk during the early years of the Google project, I suspect that the answer is, and will be, to librarians—and perhaps, especially, to librarians at the institution whose name is on the book scan. Even with the much-smaller number of University of Michigan (UM) books that were on Google Book Search in its first few years of operation, it was not at all uncommon for phone calls to come in from individuals well outside of the standard UM user base, seeking help with volumes on Google that had been scanned from UM and were marked as such on the site. Though it may require some tweaking of the mission, particularly for libraries founded to serve particular institutional and/or local communities, figuring out how to build a more targeted and useful public-service layer around these vast digital book collections will present intriguing opportunities for libraries and librarians.

THIS IS EVERYTHING, RIGHT?

It is already a commonplace that young people these days assume that any information they might need ought to be present and accessible on the Internet. As the number of books accessible online in full text expands by millions more, such assumptions will only increase. And yet, here is where that policy regime we set aside earlier comes back into play. Because, you see, if nothing changes in copyright law between now and 2020, the vast majority of books written in the twentieth century will *not* be available to read online, and there will be no way to make them so. And lest you think that I am just another copyleftist librarian striving to free all the information, I would add that those books will not be available *at any cost*: because copyright terms are so long, and because of the elimination of registration and renewal requirements, it is simply byzantine to try to figure out who might own each of those millions of copyrights—if anyone even still does. So very old books will all be out there in digital form, free for anyone to use, in as many ways as people can think of. And newer books, those in-print, in-copyright works described earlier, will also be available, though in more limited ways. (Perhaps we will have finally figured out an equitable and straightforward system of public library e-book lending by then!) But those works from the middle fifty years of the twentieth century—those books that have gone out of print, had their rights transferred this way and that, or fallen into copyright purgatory after their owners died or went out of business without specifying what should happen to them—those orphaned books will not be there. The universal library cannot be universal. Not the way things are.

For this reason, one of the aspects of Google Books that I have always liked the best is the so-called "snippet view" (Google). Snippet view is generally applied to books that might still be in copyright and had not been either opted out or included in the publisher program; all it shows is a maximum of three brief passages, each surrounding your search term. It is useless for reading and often doesn't provide *quite* enough information to tell you whether you should go find the physical book. Given that, you may be thinking, "Is she crazy? Snippet view? That obnoxious thing that shows me the book is there but won't let me actually see it?" And you're right. It's terrible. So why do I like it? Precisely *because* it shows you a little bit but not enough. Because it gives you a taste for what you could be reading, learning from, building upon, but are instead barred from using. Because it makes transparent what the current copyright regime is keeping out of circulation, keeping from serving the public good that copyright was created to promote. It reveals the impossibility of universality in the "library of utopia" (Singer; Carr). By 2020, I suspect Google will have done away with snippet view; from their perspective, it's just a bad user experience. But in its absence, how will readers know what they are missing? Or that anything is missing at all?

The library in 2020 will have been transformed by large-scale digitization. Many of those transformations will be wonderful and stimulating; others will be painful and potentially disastrous for particular libraries. And both types of change would undoubtedly be amplified by any policy change that facilitates public access to orphan works in addition to those in the public domain. But libraries are not ends in themselves; they do not exist merely to self-perpetuate. Rather, the mission of most libraries includes safeguarding and augmenting information access into the future. And if librarians believe in that mission, they should support this kind of change despite the challenges and should also support the changes in copyright law needed to magnify its effects.

Elisabeth A. Jones is a doctoral candidate at the Information School, University of Washington.

BIBLIOGRAPHY

Ann Arbor District Library. "Who We Are." 2012. Web site accessed October 2, 2012.

Band, Jonathan. "The Google Print Library Project: A Copyright Analysis." *ARL Bimonthly Report* 242 (October, 2005). PDF accessed April 5, 2006.

Becker, Samantha, et al. *Opportunity for All: How Library Policies and Practices Impact Public Internet Access*. Washington, DC: Institute of Museum and Library Services, 2011. PDF accessed October 2, 2012.

Carr, Nicholas. "The Library of Utopia." *Technology Review* (May/June 2012). Web site accessed May 1, 2012.

Courant, Paul N. "Scholarship: The Wave of the Future in the Digital Age." *The Tower and the Cloud: Higher Education in the Age of Cloud Computing*. Edited by Richard N. Katz. Washington, DC: EDUCAUSE, 2008. PDF accessed August 14, 2012.

Courant, Paul N., and Matthew Nielsen. "On the Cost of Keeping a Book." In *The Idea of Order*, 81–105. Washington, DC: Council on Library and Information Resources, 2010. PDF accessed August 14, 2012.

Digital Public Library of America. "About." Web site accessed October 1, 2012.

Duguid, Paul. "Inheritance and Loss? A Brief Survey of Google Books." *First Monday* 12, no. 8 (2007). Web site accessed May 26, 2010.

Google, Inc. "What You'll See When You Search on Google Books." 2011. Web site accessed November 11, 2011.

HathiTrust Digital Library. "Welcome to the Shared Digital Future." Web site accessed October 1, 2012.

Howard, Jennifer. "Google Begins to Scale Back Its Scanning of Books from University Libraries." *Chronicle of Higher Education* (March 9, 2012). Web site accessed March 13, 2012.

Internet Archive. "Ebook and Texts Archive." 2012. Web site accessed March 13, 2012.

"JSTOR Establishes Paper Repositories." *JSTOR NEWS* 8, no. 3 (December 1, 2004). Web site accessed October 2, 2012.

Lavoie, Brian, and Lorcan Dempsey. "Beyond 1923: Characteristics of Potentially In-Copyright Print Books in Library Collections." *D-Lib Magazine* 15, no. 11/12 (November/December 2009). Web site accessed October 1, 2012.

Library of Congress. "About the Collections." *American Memory*. Web site accessed January 26, 2011.

Nadella, Satya. "Book Search Winding Down." *Bing Community*. May 23, 2008. Web site accessed February 2, 2012.

New York Law School. "The Public Index: Amended Settlement and Responses." 2010. Web site accessed August 16, 2010.

"Opinion and Order." *The Authors Guild, Inc., et al. v. HathiTrust, et al.* 11 CV 6351 (HB). 2012.

Project Gutenberg. "About—Gutenberg." November 3, 2008. Web site accessed January 26, 2011.

"Rejected Settlement Opinion." *The Authors Guild, Inc., Association of American Publishers, Inc., et al. vs. Google, Inc.* Case No. 05 CV 8136-DC. 2011.

Rieger, Oya Y. *Preservation in the Age of Large-Scale Digitization*. Washington, DC: Council on Library and Information Resources, 2008. PAIS International. PDF accessed May 26, 2010.

Samuelson, Pamela. "Google Book Search and the Future of Books in Cyberspace." *Minnesota Law Review* 94, no. 5 (2010): 1308–74. PDF accessed May 26, 2010.

Sandler, Mark. "Disruptive Beneficence: The Google Print Program and the Future of Libraries." *Internet Reference Services Quarterly* 10, no. 3–4 (2005): 5–22. Web site accessed May 26, 2010.

Shank, Jenny. "What Is the Role of Libraries in the Age of E-Books and Digital Information?" *MediaShift: Your Guide to the Digital Media Revolution.* May 1, 2012. PBS. Web site accessed May 3, 2012.

Singer, Peter. "Whither the Dream of the Universal Library?" *Guardian*, April 19, 2011. Web site accessed April 20, 2011.

Sporkin, Andi. "Publishers and Google Reach Settlement." *Association of American Publishers*, October 4, 2012. Web site accessed October 11, 2012.

St. Clair, Gloriana. "The Million Book Project in Relation to Google." *Journal of Library Administration* 47, no. 1/2 (2008): 151–63. Academic Search Complete. PDF accessed May 26, 2010.

Wilkin, John P. "Bibliographic Indeterminacy and the Scale of Problems and Opportunities of 'Rights' in Digital Collection Building." *Ruminations* (February 2011). PDF accessed October 1, 2012.

NOTES

1. The Internet Archive's numbers are difficult to separate out from Google's because many of the volumes indexed there were actually digitized by Google and then uploaded to the IA website by entities like the Pirate Bay (IA user "tpb").

2. I am glossing over the lawsuits here, for lack of space. In brief: following the rejection of a very broad and highly controversial proposed settlement agreement in 2011 ("Rejected Settlement Opinion"), Google negotiated a more limited settlement with the Association of American Publishers in October 2012 (Sporkin). A second lawsuit, brought by the Authors Guild, still seems likely to go to court. However, given the also-recent ruling in *Authors Guild v. HathiTrust et al.*—summary judgment in favor of HathiTrust, on fair-use grounds ("Opinion and Order")—the guild's similar suit against Google may have just become much more difficult to win.

3. My involvement has stemmed from both employment at the University of Michigan (Google's largest contributor and a founding member of HathiTrust) and my own dissertation research, for which I conducted interviews with leadership of both Google Books and the Open Content Alliance. (And due to overlap between digitization initiatives, those interviews cover much of the leadership of HathiTrust and DPLA as well.)

4. In which publishers contract with Google to show book previews that go beyond fair use, as a way of selling more books (http://books.google.com/intl/en/googlebooks/publishers.html).

5. If I'm getting really optimistic, maybe Google will have donated all of its scanning equipment to libraries and/or other institutions interested in scanning, since they are no longer using it.

6. Though such materials have generally been excluded from LSDI scanning, I have some optimism about the potential for libraries to have filled in many of those gaps under their own steam in the next eight years; after all, scanning special collections was the central focus of library digitization long before LSDIs existed (see Sandler).

Chapter Four

Clifford A. Lynch

The American public library in 2020 will be a mirror of the broader society's questions and discontents about the evolution of the marketplace for cultural materials—and indeed the nature and scope of these cultural materials—in response to the growing acceptance and even embrace of networked information. It will be an institution in profound transition, rebalancing and restructuring its portfolio of services and investments.

Some things won't change much: the role of the library in helping people to access social services, to find jobs and start businesses, to acquire and refine various forms of literacy, to learn how to discover and evaluate information. Connections and partnerships with K–12 education and community colleges will continue to be important.

Physical materials—books, periodicals, videos (DVDs), sound recordings (CDs), and similar materials—will still be purchased for the library's collection and will continue to circulate as they have for decades. But in 2020, that now very large sector of library patrons who want to download borrowed e-books, music, or video onto their readers, tablets, players, or computers, either in person at the library or from home across the Internet, are likely to be disappointed. Many works, particularly the new best-selling materials from the big content providers, may simply be unavailable from the library in electronic form; patrons will have to settle for a circulating physical copy. Or the library electronic versions may come with such long wait lists that they might as well be unavailable.

And by 2020, some gaps will begin to appear in public-library collections: important works of broad public interest that are *only* available as electronic downloads but that aren't offered to libraries by their publishers in electronic form or are embargoed for long periods. In 2020, this will still be rare, at least for books in which the physical artifact is loved and honored by much of the public. Perhaps this will be much more commonplace for video and for music, but the trend line is clear and troubling. [1]

It's not clear how much damage this is doing to the public's ability to get access to information and cultural material. How many people genuinely *depend* upon the public library for access and need access to the materials that the library can't get for its collections. How much do the emerging collection gaps matter? Obviously it's annoying and frustrating for patrons when they can't download an electronic version of a work from home, and if they want to borrow from the library, they have to go there and be satisfied with physical works; this may shift some patrons to patterns of more purchase and less library use. But to what extent is this a genuine *barrier* to access? [2] It is also not clear yet how many of the patrons who can't get what they want, or, more commonly, can't get what they want in the format that they prefer, will punish their public library by voting to reduce its public financial support.

What's happened here? As content has moved to the network, it has been shifted to an economic framework based on license rather than sale. Content licensing for electronic works circumvents the traditional doctrine of first sale and related copyright provisions that allow libraries (and consumers) both to circulate and to preserve materials that they purchase in a common public market for information and cultural works. This change has allowed the major commercial content providers (particularly book publishers) to realize a very long-term objective: to totally prevent libraries from competing with their sales or to make sure that they pay for every sale that the publishers feel they have been deprived of. And some of the content providers have done exactly that, creating discriminatory pricing for library use of their works when they choose to permit such use at all under their licensing terms. Electronic public-library collections, such as they are, exist entirely at the pleasure of the content industries.

In some cases, content providers have made electronic materials completely unavailable for circulation (and preservation) by public libraries. In other cases, they've allowed libraries to acquire electronic content for circulation but under conditions that reduce its value (for example, availability embargos that keep new content out of libraries for the first six months that it's on the market) and increase its cost (for example, materials that are licensed to circulate but priced at one hundred times the cost of a personal copy in the consumer marketplace or materials that are only rented to the library for a limited time or a limited number of uses and, thus, cannot be preserved or made part of a permanent, long-term collection but are still priced at a premium to the cost of personal copies). When electronic content is available, but only under bad terms, public libraries have had to make hard choices about how much investment in electronic versions is appropriate, as opposed to investment in traditional physical materials. [3] Different libraries

have made different choices, based upon and trying to balance their understanding of the needs and preferences of their patron base, their concerns
about the importance of long-held library values involving reader privacy,
permanent collections, and preservation, and their judgments about the best
use of limited funds.

Indeed, in many ways, it's a good time to be a big publisher—along with
finally getting control of the ways libraries might acquire and use your electronic content, they've also basically eliminated the used resale market for
purely electronic content, as well as a tremendous amount of the unorganized
social sharing and lending among individual consumers that they felt used to
steal away additional sales. And there are amazing amounts of data to be had
about who is engaging and enjoying what content and how often, though it's
sometimes complicated to get this data. The only clouds on the horizon for
the publishers are that the populace overall seems to be reading fewer books,
and it's proving devilishly difficult to fully monetize content assets in the
very complex, ever-changing collection of business models and ecosystem of
aggregators, intermediaries, and others that are enabled by the Internet; profits aren't always what they used to be.

But back at the public library in 2020, there's much more going on here
than a painful and ultimately doomed rear-guard action against a marketplace
structure turning against libraries and consumers, in the face of a legal and
legislative system that's apparently unwilling to protect libraries from the
changes, no longer supporting provisions in intellectual-property law and
policy to honor and enable historic library roles (or indeed the historic purposes of copyright itself). There are signs of a series of quiet, modest revolu-
tions and shifts that will have longer-term ramifications. Public libraries in
2020 have been forced to be much less about access to current best sellers;
this creates a huge opportunity to bring other content to the attention of their
public. Smaller publishers (including mostly nonprofit publishers of academic and research materials but also vast numbers of niche commercial publishers) and a fast-growing sector of independent authors (only some of whom
are trying to make a living, or even a meaningful direct income stream, from
their writings) are negotiating comfortable and mutually advantageous arrangements to make their works available through public libraries, *particularly* in electronic versions (which are all that are offered in a growing
number of cases for these materials, since the small content creators don't
have the budget to invest in print). High profile, popular, independent authors, having broken relations with their publishers and gone to direct sales to
the public, have emerged by 2020 as a critical "swing" group; public libraries
need their works, and to some extent they need public libraries as a marketplace and as a way to find an ever-broader audience, but the negotiations are
contentious and difficult and made more problematic by the lack of mecha-

nisms for either side to negotiate at scale—too often it's still one or a few libraries talking with one or a few authors at a time.

Local connections have become particularly important and particularly vibrant: materials of local interest for historical, genealogical, or cultural reasons; local authors; local musicians and performers; documentary materials; playwrights; and partnered theatrical directors and troops. Many of these artists, creators, and scholars are seeking a public, and they have found that partnerships with public libraries, including participation in live events of various kinds hosted at the library, are very effective in building such an audience. Vast amounts of older, public-domain materials are readily available in digital form and can be explored by libraries for local relevance. And, oddly, nontextual materials have become more mainstream and more heavily used as part of the library's collection. Although the biggest textual publishers have essentially viewed libraries as enemies, this perception is less deeply held among the music, film, and video content providers, who in some cases have offered much better terms than the large book publishers. At the same time, public perceptions have changed over the past few decades: audio and video are now far more legitimate and welcome both as art forms and as vehicles for communicating information, and the historically privileged role of texts has diminished somewhat. The conjunction of good acquisition terms, changing societal bias, and changing patron preferences has altered usage patterns in unexpected ways.

There are some odd market dynamics that are starting to emerge around the edges, making the big content providers a bit nervous and keeping the consultants to these big content providers very busy: more frequently than in the past, material that did not come from these big content providers went mainstream and prominent; analyses suggest it's in large part because of the involvement (coordinated or not) of various public libraries in bringing the material into the public eye, coupled with genuine grassroots activity in the social-media sphere (as opposed to a calculated marketing campaign).

The nature of the public-library collection is changing. The role of the library is no longer to mainly provide access for well-known, new, mass-market material. Rather, the library selects material and makes a lot of introductions to less well-known content, old and new. Collections are getting larger and less volatile (no longer are such large numbers of new mass-market works acquired and then mostly discarded after a year or two); they are getting more diverse and distinctive from one public library to the next.

In recent decades, public libraries have been all about access. Stewardship and preservation of the cultural record have been mainly left to research libraries and other cultural-memory organizations, such as archives. In 2020, a series of subtle social changes is beginning to take hold that is returning stewardship to the public-library agenda. The public broadly has now recognized that a great deal of its own personal and family history is embodied in digital materials that it has come to understand are in many ways very fragile; the public is reaching out to libraries for help in organizing and curating these materials and in preserving them. Through hard experience, the public has become appropriately skeptical of having too much confidence in the stewardship commitments of commercial actors, be they sharing and social-media sites, archiving services, or content marketers. In a world where consumer products are streamed or locked to platforms such as e-book readers, where they are ephemeral and vendor dependent, we see a populace that also starts to sense how greatly mass-market cultural materials are at risk; a corporate failure, for example, might mean losing one's long-developed (and expensive) personal library of texts, music, and/or videos. They are resigned to the notion that it's unlikely they'll be able to pass these collections to their children and grandchildren (or to contribute them to stewardship organizations like libraries) in the way that earlier generations passed on physical books and sound recordings.

While they may not expect the public library to *solve* these problems, they do expect libraries to at least help. And these perceptions of fragility and ephemerality everywhere in the digital world will increase sensitivity about the fate of materials that they can control or that are controlled by sympathetic parties that share in these concerns about stewardship and continuity of access. Digital representations of the lives of local community members ("digital lives"), local history, and local culture of all kinds are becoming integral parts of public-library collections, and these public libraries are asserting and undertaking a stewardship and preservation role over these materials, even as they have been blocked from taking a similar role with regard to national and international "blockbuster" commercial-media materials, which can only be handled, to the extent that they are handled at all, by copyright deposit requirements involving national libraries or noblesse oblige–type arrangements with particular research libraries or other memory organizations.

With this new emphasis on stewardship comes a complex of new or rejuvenated alliances and partnerships. These include historical societies; government entities at the state and local level maintaining public records, particularly in electronic form, without the capability to manage these for the long term; local businesses that might want to make certain business records or databases part of the cultural record; and the local cultural heritage and arts sectors broadly. Some alliances will be more complex and include competitive elements: for example, there will be natural partnerships with universities and their libraries and archives, which bear so much of the burden and host so much of the expertise and infrastructure surrounding digital stewardship, but there will also be some amount of competition as research libraries also pursue the development of new and unique collections in the digital world; academic libraries will invoke prestige, expertise, and scholarly specialization that can be brought to the collection development and stewardship processes in place of the public library's appeal to local connections in trying to attract content. Hopefully, links, replicated copies, and other technologies will help keep the competition at a constructive rather than a counterproductive level here.

There will also be very powerful forces toward centralization or reliance upon collectives of libraries because of the economies of scale and the need for high levels of technical skills for curating digital materials; public libraries will want to rely upon and share platforms for mounting, offering, and curating digital content. Applications as network-based services, offered by organizations that the libraries trust (particularly for stewardship), will be the order of the day.

It has been clear since at least the early 1990s that the evolving Internet undermines geography as an organizing and structuring principle; futurists in those years spoke of the "death of distance." Public libraries in the United States, circulating physical object to their patrons and most often primarily funded through local taxes, have always been institutions based on geographically defined communities. It has taken the large-scale consumer adoption of network-delivered electronic content and the predictable business choices of the big content companies, combined with the Great Recession and the accompanying extraordinary public disinvestment in education and culture, to finally force public libraries to deal with many of the implications of the weakening of geography as structure. Interestingly, to the extent that popular commercial works continue to be available in public libraries only in physical form due to content-provider policies, this will serve to reinforce the old geographic models (and, in some quarters, the perception that libraries are outdated, archaic organizations). In 2020, we begin to see some public libraries grapple more seriously with serving communities of both patrons and content providers that are not necessarily defined by geographic proximity. Ultimately, it seems possible that some public libraries will move toward membership-based funding strategies as a means of financial survival, where members don't need to be in close geographic proximity; possibly the first explorations will be hybrid public and membership funding models. Of course, challenges will be raised—are these in fact public libraries or some reinvention of the historic subscription/membership model library? Do they retain the public-policy roles of traditional public libraries? Should memberships for the poor be subsidized, and if so, how?

Moving away from entirely geography-based user communities sets up new competitions among public libraries based on collections, services, and expertise (and cost) and between public libraries and other players, both commercial and noncommercial. In 2020, or shortly thereafter, these strategic questions will start to emerge in a serious way: public libraries (or former public libraries) will be exploring the range of alliances and nature of various potential specializations and making a variety of different choices about how much weight to continue to assign geographic proximity as a structural principle. One of the most interesting prospects will be the possibility—indeed, the likelihood—of library mergers or close alliances among libraries where the libraries involved are geographically distant, as opposed to the historic collaboratives made up of geographically proximate public libraries. It's not clear how this alters the negotiations for content, either from large commercial content providers or from other content creators (who may now be "local" in the sense of common interests rather than geography, if libraries are willing to specialize in appropriate ways), but it will reshape them.

Acknowledgements: I am grateful to Michael Buckland, Joan Lippincott, and Cecilia Preston for their comments on earlier drafts of this essay.

Clifford A. Lynch is executive director of the Coalition for Networked Information.

NOTES

1. What we can see emerging here is a new kind of digital divide issue: content that is *only* available in digital form, that is not made available to libraries (possibly because it's in digital form), that is costly, and that is important to the public but only available to those who are both relatively well-off and comfortable with the digital environment. This is different from the classical digital divide, which is largely concerned with important digital material that people can't get access to because of some mix of lack of expertise, network connectivity, or cost—but that the public library has been in an ideal position to help people with and where it routinely and essentially provides that help. On the bright side, in 2020, the continued drop in the price of consumer technology and the continued proliferation of at least mediocre Internet connectivity have served to whittle down some of that traditional digital divide in terms of raw access, though the effects of the Great Recession and continued problems around education and literacy among the poor have proven much more difficult to overcome.

2. There is also a "green" issue here, particularly for libraries that are not in easy walking distance for most of their patrons; as awareness of the environment and climate change grows and the perceived social cost of travel increases, the need to physically visit the library in order to transact business that in a more "sensible" world could be done over the net will be seen as increasingly irresponsible and become a target of criticism. Most likely, libraries, rather than publishers, will unfortunately bear the brunt of this criticism. In addition, the growing actual expense of the transportation involved (e.g., gas, transit fares) in the physical visit will deter borrowing.

3. Differential pricing is nothing new; academic and research libraries have suffered with this in the journal sphere for many decades (indeed even before journals went electronic), but there are important differences in the situation the public-library world faces with books. Research journals are a closed system: libraries are by far the dominant purchasers of academic journals, and most of their authors are in universities. The notion of journal publishers wholesale withholding access by refusing to license to academic libraries—opposed to extracting as much money as possible—is unlikely. Public libraries don't buy a lot of periodicals, relatively speaking, though, by 2020, they are going to find access to these growing increasingly more problematic. Important "crossover" journals like *Nature* or *Science*, that make the news and often draw the attention of the broader public, may well be priced out of the public-library market's reach. And, of course, public libraries are not the primary market for general-interest

fiction and nonfiction. (Though they argue they are a significant marketplace, too significant to ignore in the transition to e-books, based on their behavior to date, many of the major publishers don't seem to agree.) There are also examples of discriminatory pricing that have been used at various points in the evolution of the consumer video market; libraries will face challenges in this sector as well.

II

People

Chapter Five

Sarah Houghton

The library in 2020 will be ruled by geeks. In my happy vision for the future, libraries are ruled by benign geek librarian overlords, and the world is full of awesome.

Ultimately, libraries are and always have been community centers for data—the collection, classification, management, organization, dissemination of, and access to data. For hundreds of years, that meant paper, parchment, vellum, what have you. It meant physical objects in physical spaces, and it meant physical access points—log books and cards with handwritten or typed lists of the items in question. Physical objects with data expanded into multimedia, and then we saw physical objects merge into digital (think CDs, which are a digital format), and then those objects morphed into virtual objects. Now entire collections can sit on a USB drive the size of a blueberry. The Library of Congress's entire print collection could live on a bank of servers that would fit into my linen closet.

So back to the geeks. The geeks run the servers, the cloud infrastructure, and the software. They create the security that protects your users' information, and they build the platforms that allow access to the data. Geeks are familiar with the Internet tools and sites that our communities use themselves and therefore able to communicate with the community in their own spaces and their own languages. Geeks, therefore, have grown increasingly important as our users turn more and more to digital formats by preference.

WHEREFORE THIS MOVE TO GEEKERY?

The current economic crisis has fueled downscaling in almost every library—relatively expensive MLIS librarian positions have been frozen or downgraded to support-staff positions. Ask yourself this: when the economy recovers and libraries find themselves with a little more money each year, where do you think we're going to put it? Hiring a whole bunch of reference librarians they've somehow found a way to do without for the last several years (for better or worse)? Unlikely. A more plausible scenario is that we will hire geeks. We will create new positions, perhaps merged tech/MLIS positions, but tech positions nonetheless. We want and need people who can build and manage information systems, and today that means having an understanding of technology from the inside out.

We know that our populace is demanding more and more information digitally. They want information in the formats they choose, on the devices they choose, accessible anywhere they want—home, work, school, and of course mobile. Those are reasonable demands. We in libraries are sadly ill-equipped to meet them at present, due largely to the ridiculous antiquarian brouhaha that is the Digital Millennium Copyright Act and the ability of content owners and distributors to inflict restrictive terms of service on their content that disallow any library access whatsoever. This Wild West transition period is only temporary, though. By 2020, will the issue of libraries' access to digital content be resolved? I believe so. And for the sake of argument, let's assume that some forward and positive movement has been made on the issue of copyright exemptions for libraries for digital content (extended from the very same exemptions we have for physical content). In short, let's assume that libraries actually have the right to license and/or purchase all the same content that consumers do—books, audio, video, multimedia, and so forth.

As more of the data that we manage for the library moves into a purely digital format, and as we grow increasingly frustrated with the for-profit companies who provide us with platforms for that digital content (and who hire a ton of geeks, incidentally), libraries will need (let me say that again: need) people with the technical expertise to manage that content.

AND THE GEEKS SHALL RISE UP. . .

We have slowly seen geeks rise to power in libraries. Influence of the geek class has grown in all professions and in ours since the advent of punch cards, public computers in the 1980s, Internet access in the 1990s, and Web and social media in the first decade of the twenty-first century. This decade we're seeing an uptick in demand for mobile technology–savvy programmers and network specialists. The types of geeks we need change year to year, but the principle remains the same—the library cannot function any longer without its geeks, who have therefore made themselves indispensable.

We used to need geeks who could troubleshoot a printer, who could figure out how to get a stuck floppy disk out of a drive with a letter opener, who knew what defragging a hard drive was and who were willing to poke keys and buttons until something worked. Now the geeks we need are more multifaceted—we need people with user-experience training, people willing to take on risky projects, learn a brand-new just-released technology in 24 hours, program in a dozen languages, set up a secure wireless network, and design a mobile app. The skills we need change, but the geekology remains the same.

Since I became a librarian in 2001, I have seen my colleagues with technical skills become essential team members, headhunted by other libraries, and rise in influence and power within libraries of all sizes and types. Communities are starting to see more younger-than-average librarians like me with technical skills taking on administrative positions—broadening our reach and influence beyond things with bits, bytes, and cords. The techies, in short, are taking over. We're running your libraries today, and more of us will be doing so in 2020. All your library are belong to us. (If you don't understand that reference, you need to amp up your geekery.)

So why are the geeks taking over? Or, as at least one of my librarians would ask, why are the geeks being allowed to take over? The very skills that make techies good at what they do also make for good leaders—flexibility, comfort with constant change, problem-solving skills, creativity, and a willingness to constantly learn. If you've ever tried to build and launch a website from scratch or network an original Carnegie Library, you will have most of the mental skills necessary to build a new library building, launch a capital campaign, manage a large staff, wield political savvy like a whip, and eat staff meetings for breakfast.

Hiring boards and stakeholders see librarians with technical proficiency as desirable to help them build the library of the future—to keep the library not only relevant but also essential to the community. You can decide whether it's good judgment or technolust that makes people in power think that we techies will save them. The fact remains that geeks are everywhere in libraries today and more so with each new hire.

WHERE THIS WILL TAKE US

I basically see three possible futures for libraries in the broadest of strokes. Of course, some blend of these could occur and likely will . . . shades of grey being the name of the future game. But in all three futures, the geeks are the ruling class. As a side note, each scenario title is a rip off of a popular Internet meme. If you're unfamiliar with them, again—you need to amp up on your geekery.

Scenario 1: Y U No Like Library?

Libraries will become victims of their own chronic passivity and resistance to change, losing out in the public consciousness to consumer digital-content subscription services, search companies, and the idea that "free is good enough" that has invaded the school systems and people's research mentalities. As a result, there will be little love left for the library. Libraries have already seen a decrease in priority for funding and support within their parent organizations (municipalities, schools, businesses) and would continue to see further decreases. As a result, libraries will need to focus on reproving the library's value to their communities and/or to these new donors and sponsors. Focusing on the library's "from anywhere" digital impact on the community, media access, and technology skill building would be crucial in rebranding the library's worth in people's minds. A library solely based on physical space, media, and services will not be able to sustain itself in 2020 or being able to attract donors and sponsors. Digital will rule supreme, and we will need geeks to make that work.

Scenario 2: Ehrmagerd, Makers!

Users stop thinking about libraries as a place to get stuff and start thinking about it as a place to make stuff. Libraries' physical and virtual spaces will change dramatically, becoming knowledge- and art-creation centers instead of consumption centers. We're already seeing this happen with audio and video recording studios, 3-D printers, musical instruments, remixing centers, and more. For this model to be successful, we need physical and virtual technologies to facilitate our communities' creativity, as well as people to install, maintain, and train on these technologies. The library will become a host to locally created content, featuring local authors, musicians, artists, and videographers in their physical and virtual spaces, giving voice to the community within the community itself. The library can train those new to the technologies, and experienced users would have access to the advanced hardware, software, and content that they might not otherwise be able to afford access to. Public space, both physical and virtual, becomes a porous open space for creation and dissemination of community-created data.

Scenario 3: Honey Badger Does Care

The new content divide (access to digital content and devices and the knowledge of how to use them) spurs a public demand for civic services to bridge the gap, much as happened initially with the print divide spurring an interest in forming shared civic-sponsored libraries. Funding will flow like Pixy Stix at Candy Mountain. Libraries' role as providing access to information and expertise to all will be reenergized by the public realization that all this digital stuff is great but woefully unaffordable for most. Once again, as more and more content moves to the digital, we will need people to host and provide usable access points to that content and to maintain the systems that our users tell us are crucial to their information needs.

The geeks shall not only inherit the earth, they have already inherited all of its knowledge by managing all of the world's information systems. And we in libraries want geeks with the ethics and values for open information and freedom of access to be the ones in control of the world's data—in other words, us. As the type of work in libraries changes, the role of an information way-finder remains crucial as well. We need librarian techies; we need MLIS/CS degree holders. We need hybrid geeks who can offer the best of all geekery to a library—the skills to build access and the skills to facilitate and communicate with the public. In other words, we need people who can both master and excel at the technology and explain it to other people in plain language. So let's get to it and hand over control to the geeks now. It's inevitable; resistance is futile. Just give us the reins now and wait for change to hit you in the face.

Sarah Houghton is director for the San Rafael Public Library and the author of the Librarian in Black blog.

Chapter Six

Stephen Abram

The library in 2020 will be *everywhere*.

This has been the inexorable destination since the first Internet Big Bang. Of course, the library in 2020 is quite different from the librarian. The librarian will be *somewhere*—both virtual and physical. Let's look first at the changes evident in the 2020 information ecology, wrought over the past very few decades. Then I will predict the role and evolution of the librarian in 2020.

By 2020, the physical plant of most libraries has changed radically from the storage and access spaces of today. From the beginning of the Internet, we saw core strategies of libraries in the physical world under threat (and opportunity). Homogenous physical strategies became quaint if they failed to adapt to changes in user expectations that demanded experiences that matched their experiences with the consumer Web. Digitization of collections stretched the concept of "the collection" from an inventory of great content aligned with community, organizational, research, or learning goals to one where on-demand access to everything dominates. Format expectations moved from physical books, CDs, and DVDs to a hybrid hard copy and digital environment. New communication modes, from e-mail through texting to e-learning and collaboration software, stretched the boundaries of what it means to teach, answer, and relate to end users. Devices moved from being space dependent—desktop computers, home phones, movie screens, televisions, radios—to being infinitely and personally available through integrated, individual, pocket-sized smartphones and tablets that are aware of location and tuned to individual needs, as opposed to the standardized institutional needs of the host organization. Mobility rules the day. Library physical spaces are rarely dominated by collections anymore but fulfill the role of

program spaces for community activities, collaboration, creation, and training. Consider these changes that are key parts of the 2020 landscape:

- *Collections*: In 2020, we are well beyond the debates about physical and
  digital collections. Virtually everyone has some form of access to everything as both historical and current content either through their own free or
  subscription access or through collaborative, cooperative access through
  relationships with institutions, consortia, academic institutions, or employers. There is growing understanding of the difference between entertain-
  ment-based collections like fiction, video, and music versus collections of
  nonfiction books and articles, podcasts, and digital-learning objects that
  support research, learning, decisionmaking, discovery, culture, creativity,
  and invention. The divide between entertainment and the research and
  answer space is fairly clear. By 2020, a critical mass of historical out-of-
  copyright content, in most languages, has been converted. Most of the
  barriers for in-copyright content in all formats, such as DRM, pay walls,
  and licensing rules and regulations, have been addressed on an international basis. While this probably will not have been satisfied to the delight
  of all parties, there is a now a legal platform for economic success, in an
  information- and knowledge-based economy, on a global basis.
- *Access*: Digital access to content and service has changed materially. Access speed and distribution have increased and relative costs have
  dropped. Access for most consumers to the Web offers more options, and
  physically based access is largely through mobile devices, and the role
  played by libraries will be tied to three main opportunities—access to
  professional assistance and training; access to community-based resources, such as 3-D printing, holographic outputs, and experiences; and
  great experiences in the community and research commons.
- *Search*: Consumer search in 2020 has gone through a sea change. Google
  search continues to be a player in the search space as part of a multitude of
  environments that deliver a more transformative experience. Most users
  have evolved to using multiple search engines depending on the context of
  their question. Simple search is still Google and Bing-like, but users
  choose to access search engines that offer results lists that offer more
  dimensions, such as visual responses like today's word clouds and taxo-
  nomic style search suggestions as options. Search results in all spaces
  offer access to content that extends beyond websites and offer varied
  formats, including books, articles, graphics, streaming media, podcasts,
  videos, education objects, expert access, and more. After several very
  public and telling events where consumer search failed to deliver the best
  results, users are now able to separate their needs and choose consumer
  search engines or professional search engines depending upon their personal situations, needs, jobs, and sentiment. There is a plethora of options

that have expanded beyond the consumer search core, and there is a mosaic of choices for both professionals and consumers, including authoritative content and quality search, visual search, semantic search, multilingual search, sentiment searching, and demarcations between intelligence and raw-content delivery. These choices are driving high demand for advice from trained information professionals just as access to alternative music and video Web search and recommendation choices drove higher demand for Hollywood alternatives.

- *Storage*: Again, this is a key shift that started to reach public consciousness in 2012 as the "cloud." No one calls it the cloud anymore in 2020. This is just the normal mode of storage. USB drives, compact discs, and DVDs have mostly gone the way of cassettes, vinyl, and VHS and Beta tapes, which remain the choices of a small niche of nostalgia and antique collectors. People still acquire and collect, but their focus is more on access to their collection—the curation of their choices and goals—and not on physical ownership. DNA-based storage is the preferred offline backup, and shared personal collections, retailers, publishers, vendors, and libraries of all stripes are sources for everyone.

- *Payments*: Payment systems have undergone some of the most extreme changes. In 2020, we have not only seen traditional "cash" and checks become a tiny part of the payment system, we see a more dynamic system of payments and micropayments with the smartphone playing a large role as a payment device using peripherals such as we see emerging with Square today, loyalty cards like Starbucks uses, and the full emergence of near field communications (NFC) payment, comparison shopping, and loyalty systems embedded in every device. Purchasing systems within HTML5 and in-app environments will spread wildly and include cloud databases of books, articles, music, films, games, education courses, and retail choices. Libraries were challenged to moderate and balance their ethic of free of charge to include one that offers end-user choice by freeing and unfettering access to information to one where users can make their own choices about payment.

- *Devices*: In 2020, the personal device will dominate. It will track your preferences and choices, and this will challenge previously inflexible opinions about privacy and confidentiality of patron information in libraries. Adult patrons will demand choice and not accept the fettered world of 2020 antiquated library policies. Personal devices are the major shift of the past decade in that the home PC/home phone or work desktop/work landline were shared resources. At first, this drew attention to more targeted advertising, but the real change was in personalized, expert, geolocated advice, services, and recommendations. By 2020, this is moderating every experience based on our personal activities, networks, profile, and location. Coupons are just the start of this today, and this kind of personalized recommendation will move into the content space quickly with entertainment first and then targeted research and workplace interests following. Choice is driven by your employer, your communities, your access profile, and your network as well as your personal curation of your own points of view.

- *Communication*: Communication in libraries will be centered on the modern reference-interview exploration, and thousands of initiatives in virtual reference are still reaching real fruition. At this point, they are largely destination services that a user must choose to take advantage of. By 2020, these will evolve into more proactive services that are embedded into the user workplace, community, learning, and decision spaces. Access to a librarian for expert information advice and assistance will be at the point of need more ubiquitously embedded into the information and experience ecology. Some of this will be Siri-like and automated, and some will be a hybrid of predictive sources, vis-à-vis LibGuides on steroids, and some will just be passive availability just where it's needed.

- *Social Networking*: Today, nearly all social networks like Facebook, Pinterest, and Twitter are consumer-based and can potentially include everyone you choose. By 2020, these social networks will evolve to more accurately reflect your specific relationships with your network—work, classes, past employers, relatives, colleagues, acquaintances, close friends, and more. Continuous personal-learning strategies are driving this development. We already see this starting—in an automated fashion—in the latest versions of Facebook and in user-driven Google+. The core of these services are the filters and the levels of trust you hold in your various circles of contacts. As evidenced by Facebook's acquisition of Instagram and Google's attempts at a social strategy, we are more than likely to see major acquisitions, convergence, and developments in the social-networking space to drive narrower, increased dimensions, more trustworthy recommendation and sharing spaces. This will challenge and lift up library strategies in their community, learning cohort, and research-team support and partnership strategies. Libraries are social institutions, and the social software for networking and collaboration increases as a key multidimensional presence for librarians by 2020 since it represents a perfect alignment with our mission. Those libraries that leapt on the bandwagon early and evolved with their user populations thrived more quickly.

- *Programs*: By 2020, the library will be evaluated less on its collections (since it would be difficult to be much better than anyone else in a digital world) and spaces and more on its professional services and programming. In 2020, librarians are truly freed from the confines of physical and face-to-face services. Programming at libraries will vastly increase in number, and this will be supported by strategies to sustainably and scalably develop, acquire, or license virtual programming. Many libraries will offer accredited courses resulting in degrees, certificates, and diplomas. Many libraries will support and offer high-school credits, GED, and credit recovery. The mandate to support learning and the availability of cost-effective courses and e-learning technologies will drive this. This will comprise part of a national strategy to lift up the overall education of the population to compete in a more complex world where employment and the economy demand better workers. A key service of librarians in 2020 is the personal-information consultation—more far reaching than traditional transactional reference but based in the offer of transformational advice underpinned by good research and content.

- *Collaboration*: Several library initiatives, already present but nascent today, will drive the development of this world of 2020. OCLC's (Online Computer Library Center) linked data positioning is key to the development of a global architecture for information access and development. The advanced collaborative thinking, begun by projects like Library Renewal, Digital Public Library of America (DPLA), Europeana, Canadiana.org, and some major-library consortia mergers, creates the scale and cooperative vision needed to achieve success. Advocacy for libraries went collaborative too with the creation of a political action committee, EveryLibrary.org, for libraries in 2012 to escape the bonds of small local initiatives and national associations' structural limitations.

Librarians, information professionals all, have adapted, as they always have done, and continue to deliver value. Of course, that value is now based even more in personal relationships and designing experiences for target audiences of information users. As most content in 2020 is now born digital and much of the corpus of born physical content has been digitized, the need for sense makers and access to those professionals who can filter content based on alignment with user, community, or institutional needs, strategic community goals, appropriateness for task, and quality and currentness is in high demand. The cliché of the information fire hose has become a figurative Niagara Falls in 2020, and every person, business, and community who depends on information for livelihood knows and understands this. The Web of 2012 put a magnifying glass on the issue of search engines polluted by commercially tuned algorithms, search-engine optimized results, contracted-content spam, and results influenced both positively and negatively by social-network recommendations and the filter bubble. Great librarians recognized this as a once-in-a-lifetime opportunity knocking.

Therefore, in 2020, librarians have valued roles in:

- Improving the quality of questions through both interpersonal relationships and interactions as well as through good virtual-service design. Budding broadcast-search initiatives to discover "where" to search as well as

specialized native-search interfaces that meet the needs of specialized audiences have matured a great deal by 2020 from the situation today.

- Professional consultation, and to be well respected and valued for this by
  clients, as all other professions are for their business, engineering, medical, or legal advice and perspectives, is a core offering. In a world where
  information is a competitive advantage, those librarians who position
  themselves as service providers versus information servants are destined
  for success. Differentiating large demographics of broad-based "user"
  populations into service niches and individual target "clients" based on
  their needs is the key.
- Professional recommendations, moving beyond just reading or access advice but using professional judgment to assist decision makers for everything from retail purchases to research advice, through entrepreneurial and
  business support, to bulletproofing your thesis or dissertation—and beyond.
- Experts in copyright compliance, licensing, privacy, information use, and
  ethics—the lingua franca of the information age and a core organizational
  role.
- Designing experiences that are scalable and sustainable for everything
  from virtual and in-person story hours, genealogical research, information
  ethics and safe searching, homework help, coursework, and any enterprise
  that needs great information to learn and decide.
- Program development and the aligning of programs with collections,
  space, and resources to meet the strategic needs of their host organizations
  and communities.
- Custom ontologies, vocabularies, metadata, taxonomies, data mining, and
  description of content aligned with mission-critical business, learning, and
  research mandates.
- Teachers and trainers to endow clients and groups of end users with the
  skills, competencies, and awareness of when information-fluency skills
  come into play. This isn't just a role played out in one-on-one training and
  classes but also in the development of scalable e-learning initiatives tuned
  to target-population needs.
- Developing measurements and analytics for determining the return on
  investment in information, learning, and decisionmaking initiatives to
  prove the value of information interventions and professionals.

These changes were driven by changes in the consumer space—by end-user
behaviors themselves—and by thoughtful interventions to take the best of
those changes and ensure that the needs of research, democracy, decision-
making, society, and discovery continue to progress and benefit society.

By 2020, just as the financial needs at the end of the previous century
created high demand for financial advice from CPAs, MBAs and CFAs, the

demand in value and employment for professionals trained in what used to be called "library and information science" as well as computer science engineering and learning and systems design professionals has grown. Librarians are no longer just tied to physical libraries—although that will remain part of the ecosystem—but are embedded on organizational teams in all sectors.

At the time of writing, September 2012, the kids entering kindergarten today will be graduating high school in 2020, and most will enter higher education and graduate about 2025. This time horizon and these kids will see and adapt to more change in the spaces inherent to the library-value proposition than any other generation in history. It behooves us to prepare for them and consider their needs well in advance.

Lastly, I have predicted and prognosticated on the future of libraries for decades now. By my own measure, I've been reasonably accurate about the direction of the changes, and I've been pretty good at identifying the key disruptors in the library space. That said, there has always been something that has come in from left field on the fringes of technology or society that comes as a surprise. In the 1980s, I was challenged to see the long-term effects of the Web, and in the 1990s, I failed to see the full potential of social networking. I also tend to be optimistic on the timing of change. What don't I think will be a big part of library offerings in 2020? I don't believe that true grammatical translation will be ready by then. We'll still be working with translations that get the gist of it, and they won't be acceptable for professional work for the most important questions. I don't think that augmented reality will have progressed too far beyond the lab, but it shows potential. As for those glasses that give you information in real time . . . not ready for primetime. And holograms and holodecks will still be in the play space, but immersive-instruction environments, like we see today in Second Life, will be hitting the market in force.

Many libraries adapt and innovate quickly, but the adoption curve can appear immutable. I still worry about our ability to adapt with nimbleness and speed. So, what haven't I seen today that will make 2020 exciting and challenging for libraries? Can we know what we don't know?

So, in conclusion, since the library of 2020 will be *everywhere*, the next decade will be strategically challenging to librarians and our employers as we position our role in a world of ubiquitous information that threatens to drown the surfer or bewilder the diver. Can librarians be everywhere too and delight the user and deliver value too?

Stephen Abram, MLS, is vice president of strategic relationships and markets for Gale Cengage Learning. He posts regularly about information trends and user experience and behavior, as well as technology issues, at his blog, Stephen's Lighthouse.

Chapter Seven

Courtney Greene

The library in 2020 will be:

a. *In smithereens*. Along with everything else, after our robot overlords reduce all surface structures to a crumbling heap of rubble. They certainly won't welcome any smarty-pants librarians wanting them to cite their sources or giving them input on data formatting. ("Excuse me, HAL9000? You've added an incorrect and unnecessary space in subfield A.") Let's not even get started on all the other factors that seem to drive computers to go haywire and wipe out the human race, already amply demonstrated in fiction and film. Simply remember this: self-aware computers always seem cute and/or helpful in the beginning. Did you think Siri *really* couldn't understand your question? She's just getting started.

b. *In memoriam*. Yes, there will still be libraries, but they'll be a feverdream mash-up of old and new: microtechnology presented in gorgeous replicas of esteemed libraries of yore (like, say, the Bodleian or the reading room at the Library of Congress). These beautiful cathedrals to the book will come complete with wood paneling, floor-to-ceiling windows, banker's lamps, and just enough shelves artfully stocked with lovely decorative bindings, natch. They'll also deliver wireless connectivity at speeds our T1 lines can only dream about and enable all kinds of nifty, seamless interaction with patron devices. Never fear, they'll be staffed by helpful librarians carrying communicators (containing the sum of all knowledge) and wearing unitards (the final frontier). Wait, no . . .

c. *In space*. "Except Europa. Attempt no landings there" (Clarke 277).

d. *In shopping centers.* A bold new concept in libraries! We'll be more accessible than ever before—imagine a library in a mall, in an airport, perhaps even a special aisle within big box stores! "Customers" will love our new comfortable seating, coffee bars, thematic shelving sections ("hmm . . . self help!"), and convenient services: discounts and the ability to order books online to be shipped directly to their home or picked up at the counter—or best of all, synced with their device. They'll love it even more when the books are theirs to keep—just a small fee for each. And most exciting, this new library model solves all those pesky e-book problems we currently face (again, just one small fee!). Who wants to borrow when you can own?

e. *In storage.* All those books are already in Google, right? So we can just send them off to a high-tech offsite storage facility and free up the space for other purposes—comfortable seating, technology support, charging stations, perhaps even for office space on university campuses. An additional advantage to this reality: since the books are all underground in storage, they escape the fiery Armageddon discussed in option (a), enabling the human resistance army to drop not just bombs, but also *knowledge* on Skynet's horde of machine tyrants.

f. All of the above. None of the above. Next question?

All kidding aside, how *will* things be different in 2020, not quite a decade away? On the one hand, a decade is just a blip in the life of Methuselah, a 4,700-year-old Bristlecone Pine in California's Inyo National Forest (United States Forest Service). On the other, a pretty large gap stands between the three-year-old learning to read and the thirteen-year-old camped out in the YA section. Technologically, a decade can feel like a lifetime: the first iPod was released just over ten years ago on October 23, 2001 (Apple, Inc.).

So what will the library of 2020 be? In attempting to answer that question, I found myself mulling over the question of what essential elements come together to constitute a library. After all, libraries share many attributes with other types of entities: collections, technology, facilities, services, people. Just looking at that list of nouns, it might be difficult for some civilians (that is, nonlibrary types) to see what makes us different from bookstores, schools, warehouses, museums, or even coffee shops. Certainly, though, peering a few years into the future of bookstores, warehouses, and coffee shops isn't a substitute for divining the future of libraries and, with them, the future of librarianship. We know our libraries are not just buildings, although our spaces are important to us and to our constituents. Collections—although integral—don't by themselves constitute a library and cannot be the only determiner of our future. Similarly, libraries are not just technology, although technology supports and enables libraries to be what they are and to do what they do—that is, our services.

Although technology isn't, or shouldn't be, the sole driver for decision making, it certainly enables us to reenvision and reengineer *how* we do our business. Looking at some trends in library technology—from ten years ago and from now—seems like one helpful lens through which to approach the question of our collective future. At the 2002 American Library Association Annual Conference in Atlanta, Georgia, the top technology trends identified by LITA (Library Information Technology Association) panelists were OpenURL, integrated online library systems, metasearching (heaven help us), and new search interfaces, user-centered design, game technology, and infrared (LITA). Check: still talking about all of those.

Last summer in Anaheim, the panel discussed structured data, tech training, mobile thinking, transformational development, and identity crisis (Enis). A public-services librarian I may be, but having spent the better part of the last two years examining, selecting, implementing, evaluating, eating-sleeping-and-dreaming about discovery systems, I must take a moment and give an especially hearty cheer to anyone who champions structured data, richer data, data that gives us more handles to grab on to the things we are describing and thus enables us to serve them up in different ways within different contexts for our different constituent groups. However sophisticated the relevancy algorithms and myriad features of any discovery product might be, at the most basic level, these systems rely on the data we feed them. Always remember, folks: "Metadata is a love note to the future" (Kissane; Sarah [sarah0s]).

The trends mentioned are all very timely and worthy of our consideration to be sure, but the item I find particularly compelling to this discussion is "identity crisis." While the panelist was addressing the topic specifically as relates to data integrity and new publishing models—that is, there is no authority-control file for authors out there on the Internet—let's take a moment to consider it at face value, as it relates to our professional identity. In this capacity, it's not a new idea and not a new problem. How much of librarianship is what we do, and how much is how we do it? Emerging technologies—whether the typewriter or the traditional integrated library system or Twitter—have opened doors to exciting opportunities but as an end in themselves put us at risk of losing sight of the meaning of our work.

Let's take a moment and look back . . . to our future—two years, specifically: 1957 and 1968. The former saw the release of *Desk Set*, a film Internet Movie Database summarizes accurately but *most* unsatisfactorily as, "two extremely strong personalities clash over the computerization of a TV network's research department" (Lang; Internet Movie Database). For the moment, I will pass over Hepburn and Tracy, a wonderfully snappy script penned by no less than the Ephrons themselves, and some truly fabulous clothes to focus on the important thing, which is libraries. The action of the film centers on the installation of "modern technology" into a reference department, and all the attendant anxieties and disruptions resultant from the question of whether computers can replace people, lived out in the work and personal relationships of the librarians and of their clients. For brevity, I'm going to spoil it for you—computers can't replace people, although they can be wonderfully handy to have around *and* a surprisingly effective foil for a romantic subplot. Good to have that settled once and for all.

In 1968, *College and Research Libraries (CRL)* published Robert Taylor's seminal article "Question-Negotiation and Information Seeking in Libraries." A quick perusal of the other articles in that same volume of *CRL* supports my working hypothesis that everything old is new again: "Professionalism Reconsidered"; "Shared Mobile Library Collections" (aka bookmobiles); "The Bottomless Pit, or the Academic Library as Viewed from the Administration Building"; "Library Instruction for the Undergraduate"; and, last but not least, "Paperbound Books: Many Problems, No Solutions."

Taylor's article considers patron interactions both with librarians and with library systems and lays out a very helpful model of question negotiation, discussing both mediated (the reference interview) and unmediated queries. In the course of doing so, he makes some wonderful observations about libraries, their future, and their ultimate purpose.

> It is an illuminating exercise to extrapolate from present technology to describe the library of the future. . . . It is further hoped that, as a result of future investigations in this area [i.e., the relationship between library systems and library users], the evolution of libraries from passive warehouses to dynamic communication centers will be less traumatic and more effective. . . . The work described here is an early effort to understand better the communications functions of libraries and similar types of information centers, *because this is what libraries are all about*" [emphasis his]. (Taylor 178–79)

R. David Lankes, in his *Atlas of New Librarianship*, says it thus: "Libraries are in the knowledge business, therefore the conversation business" (10). In other words—people talking with other people about ideas.

Throughout his article, Taylor mentions the frustration caused to library patrons by systems and advocates that the primary consideration in building systems be the needs of end users. (On that topic, he warns, "The inquirer is only concerned with getting an answer, not with system niceties. Nor is he interested in learning and maintaining currency with a system in which only a very minor part has relevance to him." [188] Oh, snap.)

So there you have it. Libraries may have changed our methods and tools, but in the essentials, we are the same. We are collections and technologies and facilities, but mostly we are about people: services, connections, communities, knowledge, information, learning. I might go so far as to say (and I do not reference this lightly) that libraries are "of the people, by the people, for the people," and as such, I, for one, hope that they "shall not perish from the earth" (Lincoln).

Rather than trying to scry out specifics of our environment in 2020—well, hold on, I am seeing some interesting new digital collections . . . and wow! I just saw a *lot* of cardigans!—I prefer to prepare for what's coming next by focusing on the enduring value of our work. Without question, librarianship is more than just the tools we use or the technology we teach. It may look, sound, or dress a bit differently from era to era, but I posit that both its future and its foundation rely on prioritizing the personal connection.

Having begun with science fiction and postapocalyptic destruction, I shall conclude with *Pride and Prejudice* (no zombies, thank you). This exchange between Mr. Wickham and Elizabeth Bennet regarding Mr. Darcy applies equally well to libraries, their transformation over time, and whatever 2020 might look like:

> "I dare not hope,"[Wickham] continued in a lower and more serious tone, "that he is improved in essentials."
> "Oh, no!" said Elizabeth. "In essentials, I believe, he is very much what he ever was."(Austen 225–26)

Thank heaven for that. Here's to a future where we continue serving and supporting our communities through means as diverse as they: books and computers and reference librarians and catalogers and information fluency and coffee carts and collaboration spaces and story time and document delivery and technology training and archives and media and digital humanities and book talks and text messaging and responsive design and special collections and big data and typewriters and social media and quiet study and events and pervasive computing and discovery and the Next Big Thing and all the other things we do or will do in the next ten years and even with those gosh-darned e-books. Just, please: no Star Trek-ian unitards?

Courtney Greene is head of Digital User Experience at Indiana University Libraries.

BIBLIOGRAPHY

Apple, Inc. "Apple Presents iPod." October 23, 2001. Web site accessed August 14, 2012.

Austen, Jane. *Pride and Prejudice*. Edited by Vivien Jones. London: Penguin, 2008.

Clarke, Arthur C. *2010: Odyssey Two*. New York: Ballantine Books, 1982.

Enis, Matt. "LITA Talks Top Tech Trends." *The Digital Shift*, June 28 2012. Web site accessed August 14, 2012.

Internet Movie Database. "Desk Set (1957)—IMDb." *Desk Set*. Web site accessed August 20, 2012.

Kissane, Erin [kissane]. "'Metadata Is a Love Note to the Future.' #nypl_labs." Tweet, September 28, 2011, 3:58 p.m.

Lang, Walter. *Desk Set*. 1957.

Lankes, R. David. *The Atlas of New Librarianship*. Cambridge, MA: MIT Press, 2011.

Lincoln, Abraham. "Gettysburg Address—'Nicolay Copy'—Transcription." Library of Congress. Web site accessed August 20, 2012.

LITA. "Top Technology Trends, 2002 ALA Annual Conference." June 16, 2002. Web site accessed August 14, 2012.

Sarah [sarah0s]. "Metadata Is a Love Note to the Future." 2011. Flickr. Web site accessed August 18, 2012.

Taylor, Robert Saxton. "Question-Negotiation and Information Seeking in Libraries." *College and Research Libraries* 29 (1968): 178–94.

United States Forest Service. "Inyo National Forest—History and Culture." Web site accessed August 14, 2012.

Chapter Eight

Marie L. Radford

The library in 2020 will be convenient and collaborative, harnessing a broad range of mobile apps that deliver anywhere/anytime information services. It is quite dangerous, but nevertheless intriguing, to make firm prognostications about what is to come. Dangerous because, like those foretelling the end of time in 2012, short-range predictions can be embarrassing, although fortuitous, in the case of the end times not occurring. The art of projecting trends is changing rapidly. Indeed, the editors of the *Futurist* note: "The scope of the predictable universe is expanding, thanks to new tools for acquiring and measuring data. The number of people with a platform to share a prediction—a statement about what will happen to the world—has grown and will continue to grow as rapidly as the Internet" ("The Best Predictions" 2012, 28). So, let's be bold and dare to take a look into the crystal ball to see what possibilities await the world of libraries, particularly reference service, by 2020.

Reference service has already entered a renaissance, an exciting time of transition and innovation (Radford 2012; Radford and Lankes 2010). It can easily be argued that libraries have undergone more change in the past ten to fifteen years than in the past one thousand years. We already know one thing, beyond a shadow of a doubt, about the landscape in the coming years: namely that change, rapid technological change, is the number one full-gale force impacting library services today and for the foreseeable future. Networked digital devices are setting this breakneck pace, and it has been estimated that bandwidth will multiply approximately three million times through the next ten years (in mind-boggling zettabytes, that go beyond petabytes and exabytes) ("Top 10 Tech Game Changers for Next Decade" 2012). Zettabytes are mind-bogglingly large and can be equated to the data stored in 250 billion DVDs ("The Best Predictions" 2012). Within the coming years ahead, as we move toward 2020, nanotechnology is pushing the limits of smaller, faster, cheaper, and, of course, cooler, beyond anything we can imagine. This technology is already here, of course, in already commonplace gizmos and gadgets that we carry around and is largely being taken for granted.

In this time of tumultuous (yet subtly incremental) expansion of the digital world, libraries are experiencing numerous challenges, as well as opportunities, which this chapter will explore. One challenge is that libraries now exist in a world where the communication and information-seeking behaviors of library users and potential users are undergoing deep, transformational change. Their workflows and habits demand that the profession's members constantly reevaluate what we are doing and how we are doing. The need is clear for us to pay closer attention to each user's experience and predilections (Woodward 2009; Gibbons 2009).

The present reality continually challenges librarians and information professionals to adapt to: new systems, software, hardware, products, formats, virtual and social digital environments, and different types of users. These adaptations are all appearing amid a time of increasing (and competing) demands on our services. Additionally, there is the undeniably essential goal of continuing to provide excellent service during a time of economic recession, in which librarians are pushed to "do more with less." It is a bit of a paradox that during this era of diminished monetary support, demand for service has increased. Many libraries have had to contend with frozen positions, staff shortages, and deep budget cuts, while increasing the range and depth of services.

However, in many ways, these shortages have also opened the door to opportunities, as innovative service and staffing models are considered, and the growing need for greater reliance on collaboration and cooperation (Radford and Vine 2011). Leaner budgets may result in more inventive approaches, enabled by forward-looking and tech-savvy librarians who are seizing the chance to shake things up a bit, to reexamine old practices, and, perhaps, to even decide to "sundown" or discontinue some services that have become obsolete.

It is not the time to bury our heads in the sand, to continue doing things the way that we always have. A very real fear is that risk aversion, conservative thinking, and resistance to change will result in libraries becoming less relevant by 2020. Can we see "the writing on the iPad?" One way to become more open and to embrace the role of change agent is in observing the foreshadowing of the future in the trends of today and in learning about the evolving preferences of the populations we serve. Not that this is an easy feat. We sometimes already have the disoriented feeling that things are morphing, moving so rapidly that we are seeing today by way of a rear-view mirror. We know that change is accelerating, but we can, perhaps, see some inkling of the future for 2020, some glimpses just around the bend in the road ahead?

Taking a look at the bigger picture, an interesting blog posting ("Top 10 Tech Game Changers for Next Decade" 2012) listed ten trends that will be impacting our already sophisticated technological landscape. Seven of these are most relevant to the future of libraries and reference as follows:

- Nanotechnology
- HD video camera (computer "eyeware")
- 3-D scanning and printing
- Visual learning robotics
- Internet data expansion
- Voice recognition
- Eye recognition

Visual learning includes the development of computers that can "see" and "think" like humans (already present in new cars that can back into a parking space without human help). Rapid advances in voice and eye recognition will result in a disappearance/morphing of keyboards such that iPhone's Siri is seen as "merely a stop on the road to voice recognition capabilities that can create even higher degrees of efficiency" ("Top 10 Tech Game Changers" 2012). Also, the expansion of Internet data is already seen in increasing file storage and cloud computing. Imagine the library of tomorrow when instantaneous translation allows us to serve all users effectively, regardless of their native language, speech difficulties, or hearing loss. Natural language processing is making great strides, although idioms and slang continue to pose a challenge to these systems.

Another set of predictions is offered by the editors of the *Futurist*, who forecast that relatively soon, by 2015, "gamification" will drive innovation in many industries whose management teams "are all looking to increase customer feedback, employee engagement, and idea generation" ("The Best Predictions," 2012, 34) by using game-like components. Additionally, the *Futurist* finds it likely that computing devices common today (tablets, laptops, PCs, etc.) will be extinct by 2022. These will "likely be replaced by some new, yet-to-be-conceived device" ("The Best Predictions," 2012, 30), as predicted by Rama Shakla, of Intel. It is probable that the next step will be emersion in the workplace, which will become a "ubiquitous computing environment" in which almost every object offers computing access (smart lights, windows, clothing, etc.). This concept "seems to be moving closer to becoming a reality" ("The Best Predictions," 2012, 30).

To zero in a bit closer to libraries, we can look at trends in higher education. One fascinating read is the Association of College and Research Library's (ACRL) "Futures Thinking for Academic Librarians: Higher Education in 2025" (Staley and Malenfant 2010). This exploratory piece reports on research that created 26 scenarios based on implication assessment of trends in higher education that are likely to impact academic libraries and research libraries within the next fifteen years. These included: academic culture, demographics, distance education, funding, globalization, infrastructure/facilities, libraries, political climate, the publishing industry, societal values, students/learning, and technology. Experts were asked to rate these trends on their likelihood/probability of occurrence, as well as how high the impact will be. The authors recommend that those engaging in strategic-planning initiatives need to be aware of these trends, which can help in decision making and projection of user needs. Although this report was prepared for the academic environment, it is a thought-provoking read for all librarians.

An ACRL committee annually reviews imminent trends that are also affecting the prospects for academic libraries. For 2012, this committee was chaired by Lynn Silipigni Connaway of OCLC (Online Computer Library Center; who also has a chapter in this book). Their list includes: communicating value, data curation, digital preservation, flux in higher education, information technology, mobile environments, patron-driven e-book acquisitions, scholarly communication, user behavior and expectations, and staffing ("ACRL 2012 Top Trends in Academic Libraries" 2010). In 2010, this committee's work indicated that there will be a rise of the nontraditional student (e.g., part-time, minorities, older, more diverse in culture and language). The report also projected that reference-service types will continue to merge (e.g., e-mail, chat, instant messaging, texting, face-to-face) into an increasingly seamless one-stop shopping environment. Additionally, it is thought that librarians will be conducting a wider variety of outreach, including expanded community involvement ("ACRL 2010 Top Trends in Academic Libraries" 2010).

These merging service types and changing staffing trends, pointed out by ACRL, are worth additional discussion. There are a variety of reference service models that are being implemented in a number of different types of libraries, including back-to-the future models as well as newer configurations, such as: the one-desk model (i.e., all services from one desk), hybrid model (i.e., combining one or more services, such as circulation, IT, and reference), two- or three-tiered model (e.g., information desk, reference desk, and referrals for in-depth appointments), roving reference (with or without a physical reference desk), and the call-center model (in which phone and e-reference are done from a central location, away from the physical desk) (Radford and Vine 2011).

Staffing trends are part of a major impact brought about by the Internet, according to the Pew Internet and American Life project, that has to do with a radical change in the workplace. Pew experts Mark O'Brien of the Aerospace Corporation and Ted Christensen of the Arizona Regents University have predicted that there will be sweeping changes in work environments and in how the individual performs the ways in which work is done (http://www.pewinternet.org/). One impact on libraries might be increasing opportunities for "work-shifting," in which people work hours outside of the nine-to-five model and also increasingly (and transparently) provide services from home or the coffee shop (e.g., offering virtual reference services or out-sourced cataloging from anywhere) and conduct a larger variety of outreach, including expanded civic involvement and being more deeply embedded in academic courses or community organizations.

Libraries are also being affected by next-generation search developments, such as the BiblioCommons catalog that the New York Public Library has implemented (http://nypl.bibliocommons.com). This catalog uses social-media enhancements to include greater opportunity for users to comment on holdings, to create (and share) their own reading/viewing lists, and to recommend titles. It includes a mobile app for iPhone, Android, and mobile Web that allows for cell phone and tablet access (http://www.nypl.org/mobile). Social catalogs will empower reader's advisory and recommender services, which, in company with enhancements such as LibGuides (http://springshare.com/libguides/), will result in greater discoverability, especially for underutilized items.

The killer app for libraries is still to be invented, but we can be assured that the killer technology leading to 2020, and perhaps beyond, is the mobile phone/PDA coupled with portable wireless services. Although we can be relatively sure of this, we may not be quite so sure of how precisely these will be used. Young people are leading in finding new ways to use mobile phones. We are already in the era of "4G," fourth-generation phones that connect to several wireless technologies and move seamlessly between them, and 5G devices, which enable more morphing and merging of a vast array of mobile apps. An example from the library world can be found in the Consortium of Academic and Research Libraries in Illinois (CARLI), in which their "text me this call number" widget enables users to search the online catalog and then enter the library with call number in hand(held). According to Courtney Greene, head of Digital User Experience (DUX) at Indiana University Libraries, this app has been readily adopted by users and has the potential to increase circulation of print and other materials. With the further development of augmented reality (AR), the user could use his or her phone to follow a virtual yellow-brick-type path to the item upon entering the physical building. This path could lead right to the book in the stacks, which then might light up (using radio-frequency-identification technology) and automatically check itself out to the user when he or she carries it out of the building. Or, if it is an electronic item, it could automatically download itself.

Technology will also allow new ways to evaluate reference services. For example, Amanda Cukrowicz of Indiana University–Bloomington (IUB) reported in the library blog (https://blogs.libraries.iub.edu/redux/2013/01/04/ tagxedo-a-word-cloud-program/) that she uses the Tagxedo (http://www.tagxedo.com/) word-cloud program to analyze interactions from their online chat service and reference-desk log. She then compares these from different points in the semester to find trends or anomalies in the questions being asked at both service points. IUB also uses geo-locative technology for a mobile app that tells students which university library is nearest and also which one is currently open (important information, not previously available without a phone call!) The emergence of socio- and geo-locative technology is an area that could connect electronic and physical resources much more easily for all types of libraries (Farkas 2010).

Social media is also opening up a new range of collaborative solutions to the age-old "lone ranger" one-to-one reference-service model (see also Radford 2008). The research project: "Cyber Synergy: Seeking Sustainability through Collaboration between Virtual Reference and Social Q&A Sites" (Radford, Connaway, and Shah 2011–2013), funded by a $250,000 grant from the Institute of Museum and Library Services, is investigating the possibility of opening up reference to crowd-sourcing among subject-specialist librarians and even, perhaps, credentialed subject experts who are not librarians. This is one intriguing vision for the future of virtual reference, one that is more collaborative and that strives to provide easy, seamless access to human expertise that goes far beyond that of search engines, even Google.

A future brand for librarians could be: "Convenient, free, anytime/anywhere access to information experts who care." The good news is that librarians already have the skills that it takes to be successful in the future. Our service is value-added, and it does matter. What does this mean?

- Every interaction provides excellent service to our users.
- Every user is privileged.
- Every librarian/library fully accepts the challenge to make this happen.

Clearly, there is a caveat to the future that is envisioned here. There exists a challenge to each of us to become both managers of incremental change, as well as change agents. The most vital skill going forward is the ability to thrive with change, not just to sit back and watch or fret or frown upon new initiatives. Ultimately, the future of libraries and of reference service, in whatever mode it is delivered, is up to us to create. For those on the frontlines, we are sculpting the future in the quality of the service we provide, in the decisions we make, in daring to take risks, and being ever open to learn new tricks. For researchers and library educators, impact will be made in the problems we choose to address, in the solutions we discover, and in the design and provision of a forward-looking curriculum that equips MLS students with a positive attitude, curious spirit, and, yes, traditional service values.

Marie L. Radford is chair, Department of Library and Information Science, School of Communication and Information, Rutgers University.

BIBLIOGRAPHY

"ACRL 2012 Top Trends in Academic Libraries." *C&RL News* 73, no. 6 (June 2012): 311–22.

"ACRL 2010 Top Ten Trends in Academic Libraries." *C&RL News* 71, no. 6 (June 2010): 286–91.

"The Best Predictions of 2011." *Futurist* 46, no. 1 (January/February 2012): 28–39.

Farkas, Meredith. "Guided by Barcodes: QR Codes Link Patrons to the Library." *American Libraries*, July 22, 2010.Web site accessed February 7, 2013. http://americanlibrariesmagazine.org/columns/practice/guided-barcodes.

Gibbons, Susan. L. *The Academic Library and the Net Gen Student*. Chicago: ALA, 2009.

Radford, Marie. L., ed. *Leading the Reference Renaissance: Today's Ideas for Tomorrow's Cutting Edge Services*. New York: Neal-Schuman, 2012.

Radford, Marie. L., Lynn S. Connaway, and Chirag Shah. *Cyber Synergy: Seeking Sustainability through Collaboration between Virtual Reference and Social Q&A Sites*. 2011–2013. Web site accessed February 7, 2013. http://www.oclc.org/research/activities/synergy.html.

Radford, Marie L., and R. D. Lankes, eds. *Reference Renaissance: Current and Future Trends*. New York: Neal-Schuman, 2010.

Radford, Marie. L., and Scott Vine. "An Exploration of the Hybrid Service Model: Keeping What Works." In *Reference Reborn: Breathing New Life into Public Services Librarianship*, edited by Diane Zabel, 79–89. Santa Barbara, CA: Libraries Unlimited, 2011.

Staley, David J. and Kara J. Malenfant. "Futures Thinking for Academic Librarians: Higher Education in 2025." Association of College and Research Libraries, June 2010. Web site accessed February 7, 2013. http://www.ala.org/ala/mgrps/divs/acrl/issues/value/futures.cfm.

"Top 10 Tech Game Changers for Next Decade" Good/Intel blog post, June 21, 2012. Web site accessed February 7, 2013. http://www.good.is/post/the-top-10-technology-game-changers-for-the-next-decade/.

Woodward, Jeannette. *Creating the Customer-Driven Academic Library*. Chicago: ALA, 2009.

Chapter Nine

James W. Rosenzweig

The library in 2020 will be an information base camp—a forward outpost serving as a temporary home to people journeying out into the information environment. Librarians will increasingly act as guides, experienced climbers who have the skill and the leadership ability to assist others in their trip up the mountain and back. This kind of transformation will require libraries and librarians to revise their images of themselves, but I can see this work happening already in libraries across the country, and I am confident that the profession is ready for a change.

The previous model of the library is in some ways more analogous to an indoor climbing wall. Prospective climbers came to us because we had the information environment they wanted. We controlled access to the environment, and to some extent controlled the complexity of accessing it—an easy climb here on the left, a more expert path here on the right. The information inside that library building was behind a gate we tended. The flow of information inside that space was largely limited to a conversation between two people: an individual climber would work with a librarian, who would advise them on the right path to take and then be close by throughout the entire effort. In case of a slip, we were ready and clipped in to the safety harness. Even though the world of information has changed much in the last few decades, many librarians still feel like indoor climbing instructors. We try to convince people that climbing in our library is safer and better than the dangerous mountains out there—the Googles and Wikipedias that are so unstable, so unpredictable.

It's that dynamic that has me convinced we need to reinvent ourselves as base camps, out there in the high country where people want to go climbing. The information environment is as changeable as a mountainside—shifting conditions make it easy to accomplish what would have been hard yesterday or unexpectedly challenging to make any progress researching a topic that once seemed simple. The average person is unaware of how rapidly the difficulty of a search increases and often has little specific training in how to conduct a search effectively. An individual must learn how to assess reliability of a wide array of sources to understand the differences between kinds of search tools or documents, and to determine the best means of reaching the information that satisfies his or her need. This is a situation that begs for guides: people need someone with experience to prepare and educate them, to go with them along the way, and ultimately to help them up the mountain. With time, novices will become veterans who no longer need help with routine tasks; however, the nature of this new environment means that few will ever choose to climb alone without the benefit of the latest information about conditions that is available in the conversations at base camp. The library will become a permanent way station on a busy trail.

This transformation will require librarians to adapt to some new realities, primarily the fact that much of the information environment is not under our control any longer. We haven't given up all responsibility for maintaining access to reliable information, but we need to recognize that our job isn't to convince people not to use the world of information we don't control or maintain. Some people may be satisfied with the indoor-climbing-wall experience, but many more will want to climb mountains, and we need to be out there with them. This requires us to make ourselves comfortable with that environment and to be sensitive to the subtle weather changes online that will affect the experience for the people we're guiding. We'll also need to recognize that, in this environment, we won't be the only experts on hand. There will be other guides or veteran climbers willing to offer advice and insight. We need to make the library into the kind of base camp where these people gather and converse, swap stories about new and rewarding routes to the answers they seek, and add to our expertise by sharing observations about the information environment that we haven't picked up on yet. Over time, the most important voice in any given conversation in the library will often not be our own, as community organizations, support services, and related resource professionals integrate into our space, to create the breadth and diversity of knowledge that's needed to maintain a well-informed understanding of the weather our patrons are climbing through.

The work of reimagining ourselves is already under way. In academic libraries like mine, work has been under way for several years to radically reorganize library spaces. The rise of the "information commons" or "learning commons" is an encouraging example of what a base camp library will be like—a place for sharing information freely, for learning about other peoples' research successes, and for being inspired to try new approaches. These spaces communicate new ideas about what a library is and does and about who librarians are and what they do. My only concern is that the conversations surrounding these new commons spaces still seem to envision them as adjunct elements to the larger library. They can come across as specially set-aside rooms that have very little to do with the traditional center of the library: the rows and rows of bound periodicals and monographs. The step we must take by 2020, and that I believe we will take in these coming years, is to make that commons approach the heart of the library. The bound periodicals and monographs retain their value, but we need them to become connected organically to the new library. This will require us to be thoughtful about the purpose of the commons space and the purpose of the print collection and how to integrate the two in a way that takes advantage of the strengths of each one. We will also need to reinvent library services in this new context, recognizing what will change about our patrons' needs and what will remain the same and acknowledging that the services provided in the commons environment will not always outwardly resemble our current services, even though our goals on a conceptual level will remain consistent. The point is not to simply enlarge the commons in square footage but to expand the idea of the commons to weave together the whole world of information reachable via the library. We cannot continue to run the library as a house divided: it doesn't serve our existing patrons well, and it doesn't establish a clear course for the future.

Although I've been focused on academic libraries up to this point, I should emphasize that I think this revised identity for the library will be necessary to libraries of virtually every type, serving virtually every community. School libraries, for example, have perhaps suffered most from the shifting information environment: in an era of budget cuts, it's apparently easy for many administrators to think that "the kids hardly look at books anymore." For this reason, it is especially vital that the school library be reinvented, both as a place and as an online portal, and that librarians use this new identity to advocate aggressively for the importance of teaching children and young adults how to safely and effectively traverse this new landscape. No school librarian needs to be told that this transformation is important, but a new framework for structuring the school library and articulating its mission will help make the message come through more clearly. An archives or rare-book library, on the other hand, might see this changing environment as something external to the specialized and controlled world of information inside its four walls. But, to me, one of the great challenges for these libraries will be to tie themselves to the larger conversation occurring online—to make archives seem less like dusty relics and more like vital resources in an information world that is both virtual and physical. This adaptation is already occurring, with many special libraries extending digital collections into the Web and making over their physical spaces to serve new patrons and new kinds of questions, but a lot of work remains to be done by 2020.

We cannot pretend that this transition will come easily because the newly hired librarians will bring with them to the profession this new vision for libraries. It is vitally important that existing librarians, many of whom were trained for the libraries of decades past, take on the challenge of not merely catching up to the technical proficiency of our patrons but also moving beyond them. We have long accepted that some librarians need technological proficiency; it is time to confront the truth that almost all librarians need to aim for an exceptional level of skill. No novice climber would entrust themselves to guides who admitted they don't really understand how to use all this new safety gear or who have never summited a mountain like this one before. And although it may seem I'm concerned primarily with the generation of librarians who preceded me, I know my generation of librarians well enough to know that we have our own hurdles to clear. Some of us became librarians because we believed the library was the last refuge away from all this technology—a haven for book lovers where we could live out our days in anachronistic comfort. Almost all of us came to librarianship thinking primarily of how libraries have been and what they have meant to us in the past, rather than approaching the field with a clear vision of its future. The work of remaking the image of the library in society's eyes begins with remaking it in our own. We must be willing to lose some of the things we loved most about the libraries we remember fondly if we're going to build libraries that will be truly memorable and valuable to the people we serve in the years ahead.

At the same time, it's critically important that we defend the core values of traditional librarianship and the truth that the profession we have built over a century and a half is more relevant today than ever before. Our traditional work—providing attentive personal service, using our skill to make documents more available and better organized, defending the right of privacy and the right of free access to information, and so forth—will be revitalized by the coming transformation. As we step away from our identity as gatekeepers, authorities installed behind massive and permanent desks, and into our identity as guides who go with patrons out into the world, we will discover that the talents we have long honed are useful in dozens of new settings. The demand for agility, for flexibility, and for a rapid response to the world as it is will drive us to new levels of creativity in adapting these traditional skills and help us redefine what it means to be a community's librarian. This new definition will always be informed by our past and a legacy of service we can be proud of, but it has to move forward to keep pace with the world we serve.

That move forward is why the idea of the information base camp appeals to me as a model for the library in 2020. In a base camp, expertise is decentralized, as guides share information and even learn from veteran climbers who have their own experiences to draw from. That decentralization will feel risky at first, as though we are relinquishing our status as information specialists, but I am confident that in the long run only our willingness to take that risk will cement our long-term status as experts in this new environment. It's time to show that our skills are by no means outdated, that to the contrary, we are prepared to be leaders in the twenty-first century, as fit intellectually for seeking and finding information in this environment as a climbing guide is fit athletically for scaling a challenging mountainside. Even as we alter the way we interact with our patrons, exchanging passivity for action, welcoming in the chaotic online world of information rather than trying to keep it out, our core identity as librarians will remain the driving force behind every step.

James W. Rosenzweig is education librarian at Northeastern Illinois University.

III

Community

Chapter Ten

Michael Crandall

The library in 2020 will be your best friend.

But you may not recognize it.

Over the past 30 years, we have lived through a remarkable transformation in the world of information, moving from scarcity to abundance, difficulty of access to too much access, centralized publishing to self-publishing. The rise of Internet-based services like Google, Amazon, and many others have given us "information at our fingertips" at unprecedented speed and volume. What has happened with libraries in this transformed world? Many of us probably don't even think of them when we look for information any more, or as OCLC's (Online Computer Library Center) study of public perceptions of libraries found in 2010, we think of them as essentially warehouses for books (De Rosa 38). Public libraries in particular, because they are funded as a public good, like education and fire protection, have suffered because of this perception, with the conventional wisdom often being that because we can get information so easily now we don't need libraries anymore.

But a closer examination of what is actually happening in public libraries tells a radically different story, one that is having major impacts on both the developed and developing world. For many years now, public libraries have been transforming themselves as rapidly as the commercial information infrastructure we now take for granted in the developed countries and responding to the changes in ways that reemphasize their importance to communities of all kinds.

For instance, consider the move from print to electronic books. A recent study by the Pew Internet and American Life Project on the use of e-readers and libraries found that most people in the United States don't realize that public libraries now loan e-books (and often e-readers) as well as printed books (Zickuhr 5). Yet in Seattle, Washington, over 25,000 e-books are now available to users through the public library at no charge, with additional electronic content in the form of audio books, music, and videos on top of that ("Kindle Users"). This transition to new media is not new for libraries, however, and is merely a reflection of changing delivery formats that have been going on for as long as libraries have been in existence; after all, libraries made the transition from the scrolls of Alexandria to the familiar codex form of storing content, not to mention more recent transitions involving information stored on microfilm, videocassettes, audio tapes, compact discs, and now online content of all types. Transitions in the form and substance of collections is not unknown to libraries, and today they are more agile and better equipped with tools to enable them to keep collections current and relevant for their users.

Public libraries have also been aggressive in providing alternative access mechanisms, leading the way in developing public-access computing services that are free for all users in communities they serve (and visitors as well). Virtually every one of the 9,225 public-library systems in the United States provides free access to the Internet on public terminals today. Those public Internet terminals are in high demand at most libraries—a recent study found that 32 percent of the American public ages fourteen years or older have accessed the Internet using a library computer or wireless network in the past twelve months (Becker 32). Close to two out of three Americans also access library services and the Internet beyond the walls as well through the virtual services libraries provide through their websites, such as the online catalog, subscription databases for articles, and digital books and other media (Becker 28).

This same study found that many of the users of public access technology in libraries are not just looking for books but also actively pursuing life activities (Becker 5). As can be seen in figure 10.1 (Becker 5), users of the library computers were looking for work, doing homework and taking online classes, talking to their friends and family, looking for health information, using government and legal services, and managing their finances. Given that 22 percent of these users had no other access (Becker 38), this is clearly an important resource for them in the modern world.

But the real value that many users find in the public library beyond access to information is the assistance from trained professionals who can help guide people through the changing landscape of information access in the digital world. Not everyone is digitally fluent, and having a resource at hand that can help navigate the intricacies of using a computer or the Internet, assist in the process of finding and applying for a job, or show where to look for health-care assistance is a major boon for many. In the United States, the study mentioned earlier found that fifty-two million people got help using computers from a librarian or library volunteer in the preceding twelve

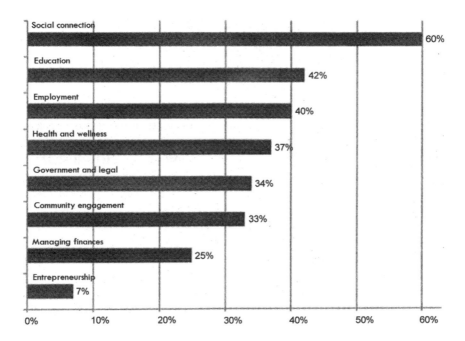

Social connection — 60%
Education — 42%
Employment — 40%
Health and wellness — 37%
Government and legal — 34%
Community engagement — 33%
Managing finances — 25%
Entrepreneurship — 7%

0%   10%   20%   30%   40%   50%   60%

Figure 10.1.

months (Becker 42). Hoffman (6), in a national survey of U.S. public libraries, found that over 90 percent of public libraries offer some type of formal or
informal technology training for patrons struggling to keep up with the ever-
changing skills needed to effectively use technology. As one user put it, "If
you run into a problem, you can go to the help desk and they would help you,
they'd walk you through step by step which is another good thing because
you got hands on here. At home, if you run into a problem, who are you
going to turn to?" (Becker 42).

This role of the information *infomediary* is something that librarians have
always provided, no matter how the information is delivered. With the added
layer of technology needed to navigate an already complex information landscape, the librarian's role as a guide and best friend is becoming increasingly
important. A soon-to-be-completed study by the TASCHA (Technology and
Social Change Group) research group at the University of Washington examines the role of these infomediaries in public libraries and other access points
around the world where Internet access is not as ubiquitous as in the United
States ("Infomediaries"). In these areas, libraries and other infomediaries
may play an even more important role in not just connecting individuals to
the information they seek but also connecting entire communities to the
wider world. Results from this study and the larger study (funded by the Bill

and Melinda Gates Foundation and the International Development Research Centre) looking at the impact of public access through libraries and other public venues throughout the world are just now becoming available and reinforce much of what has been found in the United States about the role libraries play for individuals and communities ("Global Impact Study").

Libraries are also reaching outside their walls to deliver services to areas that may not have direct access to physical space or lack an Internet connection. Recent examples outside the United States of creative ways of reaching people who need these services include an elephant library in Thailand that travels the hill country to deliver access to forty-six villages that would otherwise be cut off from the world (UNESCOPRESS) and a boat library in Bangladesh that travels the waterways to reach rural villages cut off from the Internet and other information services ("2005 Access to Learning Award"). In the United States, public libraries are moving outside their walls as well and partnering with other community organizations to provide services where people congregate, such as the hot spots offered by the Free Philadelphia Library ("Free Library Hot Spots").

The role of the library as a leader in this area has been recognized through work done recently by the Institute of Museum and Library Services to build a framework for digitally inclusive communities ("Proposed Framework"), which offers a blueprint for communities wishing to bring the major players together in shaping their digital future. Libraries are taking a lead role in the United States in moving this framework into practice through a grant funded by the Institute of Museum and Library Services (IMLS) and led by OCLC's WebJunction to teach public libraries how to take the lead building coalitions and partnerships to ensure their communities have the access, content, and skills they need to take advantage of the opportunities available through digital inclusion ("IMLS Awards Grant").

Public libraries are also going beyond passive information delivery and finding new ways to engage people in creating their own information and content, through programs such as the Chicago Public Library's YOUmedia project ("About Us") and the Fayetteville Free Library's Fab Lab ("FFL Fab Lab"), where users can engage with technology of all kinds, ranging from video to music to computers, gaining the confidence to become citizens of the information age in a supported, safe environment.

The Aarhus Public Library in Denmark is one example among many of how far this community engagement can go—over the past few years, they have asked all the citizens of Aarhus ("Transformation Lab") to help envision the future of their library through interactive exhibits and sessions in the library, exploring the use of technology and space to find what works best for learning and information delivery (children asked to have the sounds of trees coming from the shelves where books about forests were held). Aarhus is now taking this one step further and has been leading a citywide planning team that is redeveloping the waterfront area to provide an urban hub, with the library center stage as a reimagined Urban Mediaspace ("Urban Mediaspace Aarhus").

At the Beyond Access Conference (one of a continuing series of gatherings all around the world), librarians from the more than 230,000 public libraries in developing and transitioning countries across the world spent two days hearing about innovative approaches such as these and brainstorming other ways to move libraries into the future as part of strong communities ("Beyond Access Campaign"). The focus was on finding ideas and practices that could help in development of their communities through hearing directly from the practitioners and leaders who are making these things happen across the globe.

Chrystie Hill, a passionate advocate of libraries and their role as central community-center points, asks "When everything is online, why come to the library at all?" and urges us to take the steps that Aarhus did in reimagining what public libraries will be in the future (Hill). The many ways in which public libraries have already taken up this challenge and found the resources in spite of dwindling budgets to deliver critical services to all of us clearly demonstrate that there are many reasons to come to the library, whether we do so virtually or in person, and to make sure that the public library stays a part of our community, even if it may not look like what we are used to from our past experience. We all change with time, and libraries are no different—but the true value of best friends is that they continue to give us what we need no matter what the circumstances, and public libraries are indeed the best of friends in this way, now and in 2020.

Michael Crandall is a senior lecturer at the University of Washington Information School.

BIBLIOGRAPHY

"2005 Access to Learning Award: Shidhulai Swanirvar Sangstha." Bill and Melinda Gates Foundation. Web site accessed October 6, 2012. http://www.gatesfoundation.org/atla/Pages/2005-shidhulai-swanirvar-sangstha-bangladesh.aspx.

"About Us." YOUmedia Chicago, Harold Washington Library. Web site accessed October 6, 2012. http://youmediachicago.org/2-about-us/pages/2-about-us .

Becker, Samantha. *Opportunity for All: How the American Public Benefits from Internet Access at U.S. Libraries.* Washington, DC: Institute of Museum and Library Services, 2010.

"Beyond Access Campaign." Beyond Access. 2012. Web site accessed October 6, 2012. http://www.beyondaccess.net/ .

De Rosa, Cathy, Joanne Cantrell, Matthew Carlson, Margaret Gallagher, Janet Hawk, Charlotte Sturtz, Brad Gauder, Diane Cellentani, Tam Dalrymple, and Lawrence J. Olszewski. *Perceptions of Libraries, 2010: Context and Community: A Report to the OCLC Membership.* Dublin, OH: OCLC, 2011.

"FFL Fab Lab." Fayetteville Free Library. Web site accessed October 6, 2012. http://www.fayettevillefreelibrary.org/index.php/about-us/services/fablab.

"Free Library Hot Spots." Free Library of Philadelphia. Web site accessed October 6, 2012. http://www.freelibrary.org/libserv/hotspots.htm.

"Global Impact Study." TASCHA, University of Washington, Seattle. Web site accessed October 6, 2012. http://tascha.uw.edu/projects/global-impact-study/.

Hill, Chrystie. "Libraries Present and Future." TEDxTalks. December 28, 2011. Web site accessed October 6, 2012. http://www.youtube.com/watch?v=ohKEWTXk0F8 .

Hoffman, Judy, John Carlo Bertot, and Denise M. Davis. "Libraries Connect Communities: Public Library Funding and Technology Access Study 2011–2012." *American Libraries*, digital supplement, June 2012. Web site accessed October 6, 2012. http://viewer.zmags.com/publication/4673a369 .

"IMLS Awards Grant to OCLC's WebJunction to Get Communities on the Path to Digital Inclusion." OCLC, November 15, 2011. Web site accessed October 6, 2012. http://www.oclc.org/news/releases/2011/201167.htm .

"Infomediaries: Brokers of Public Access." TASCHA, University of Washington, Seattle. Web site accessed October 6, 2012. http://tascha.uw.edu/projects/infomediaries-brokers-of-public-access/about/ .

"Kindle Users Now Have Access to E-Books at the Seattle Public Library." Seattle Public Library. Web site accessed October 6, 2012. http://www.spl.org/about-the-library/library-news-releases/kindle-e-books-921 .

"Proposed Framework for Digitally Inclusive Communities: Final Report." Washington, DC: Institute of Museum and Library Services, 2011.

"Transformation Lab—Prototyping the Future." Transformation Lab, May 7, 2007. Web site accessed October 6, 2012. http://www.youtube.com/watch?v=TpFO_L_jA1c .

UNESCOPRESS. "Laureates of UNESCO Literacy Prizes 2002." Press release 2002-43. Web site accessed October 6, 2012. http://portal.unesco.org/en/ev.php-URL_ID=4091&URL_DO=DO_TOPIC&URL_SECTION=201.html .

"Urban Mediaspace Aarhus." Aarhus Kommune. Web site accessed October 6, 2012. http://www.urbanmediaspace.dk/en .

Zickuhr, Kathryn, Lee Rainie, Kristen Purcell, Mary Madden, and Joanna Brenner. "Libraries, Patrons, and E-Books." Washington, DC: Pew Internet and American Life Project, 2012.

Chapter Eleven

Molly Raphael

The library in 2020 will be *essential* for the *success* of its *community*. It will achieve this lofty position through:

- authentic community engagement
- collaboration and partnership with key community entities
- responsive services and programs that embrace the diversity of the community served
- willingness to lead change and take risks
- effective, community-led advocacy

Libraries of all types will have to adapt, not just respond to but also lead change. The rapid pace of change will require libraries to be nimble, to build strategic alliances, and to build inclusive and welcoming environments, both virtual and physical. Libraries that do not embrace these strategies will find themselves more and more marginalized, with corresponding decreases in use and funding.

AUTHENTIC COMMUNITY ENGAGEMENT

What do we mean by "authentic community engagement," a concept articulated and developed by Richard Harwood? Harwood talks about how we must "turn outward" for authentic community engagement, turning away from focusing on our programs and initiatives and instead reorienting our focus on community. Authentic community engagement means listening to community as well as including stakeholders in how we develop, modify, and deliver our programs and services. When we engage authentically with our community, we see our services through the eyes of the various parts of our communities rather than seeing members of our community as consumers of our goods and services. We help build the fabric of our community, always asking how we are contributing to the success of our communities. We look at our community and consider the individuals who make up the community, the subgroups within the community, and the community as a whole. Our work focuses on the aspirations and priorities of our communities rather than on the needs. As we build and strengthen activities based on turning outward, people at all levels within our communities see us as central to their lives and essential for their success.

COLLABORATION AND PARTNERSHIP

Libraries of all types have experienced the value of doing our work with others. In fact, collaboration and partnerships have clearly become critically important to working effectively within communities. In public libraries, we have built partnerships with businesses and economic development organizations to support workforce development. Libraries collaborate with healthcare entities to develop public health-education programs around issues such as the impact on communities of chronic diseases, the value of reducing risky behaviors, and generally improving health outcomes. These initiatives are based on health concerns central to the community served. Academic and school libraries build collaborations around priorities that are central to the institutions and communities they serve, such as how to make their resources more accessible to the students, faculty, and other stakeholders. Special and research librarians embed themselves in the work of their parent organizations, providing expanded opportunities for connecting the librarian's expertise and knowledge to constituents who are also engaged in work essential to accomplishing the organization's mission.

When we engage authentically with our communities, we can identify logical partner organizations, including both for-profit and not-for-profit entities, that share commitments to the priorities of the respective communities.

RESPONSIVE SERVICES THAT EMBRACE DIVERSITY

We are experiencing dramatic changes in the diversity of populations in our communities, at all levels and all across the country. Not so long ago, many areas of the United States had relatively homogeneous populations, but that has changed significantly in the past few decades. In addition, as the world in which we operate every day becomes more and more global, we can only become successful if we embrace the diversity in our communities and libraries. How we adapt in this global environment will be central to our thriving in the future. Libraries have been leaders in transforming services and spaces for celebrating that diversity, helping to create better understanding and contributing to how each community and individuals from diverse backgrounds can contribute to moving communities forward.

A key to success continues to be focusing on making our library workforce more diverse. The American Library Association's Spectrum Scholars initiative, providing scholarships for persons from underrepresented racial and ethnic groups to pursue master's degrees in library and information science, must continue to help bring persons from diverse backgrounds to librarianship. Many other parts of the larger library community have embraced enhanced diversity as well, such as library and information science schools, which supplement the Spectrum funding with matching scholarship programs. In addition, many libraries encourage and support their own employees from diverse backgrounds who are working in library support-staff positions to pursue master's degrees. Efforts such as these are leading to library staff being more inclusive and reflecting the diversity of the communities they serve.

We have much more work to do, however, in identifying and attracting future librarians from diverse backgrounds. An initiative launched in 2010 by the American Library Association, funded through the Institute of Museum and Library Services (IMLS) Laura Bush 21st Century Librarian Program, supports a three-year project to recruit ethnically diverse high-school and college students to careers in libraries.

Libraries also invest in training and education to improve the cultural competencies of all of their staff. Some libraries have built cultural-competency elements into their employees' performance plans and annual performance evaluations, affirming the importance of developing employees in this increasingly important area of their work. Improving cultural competencies throughout the library workplace is also key for the success of libraries in the future.

LEADING CHANGE AND TAKING RISKS

The pace of change is accelerating so rapidly that we have to be willing to take risks not only when developing and transforming our services but also in redefining our roles. We cannot just hold onto the things we like to do or the things that we studied in library school years ago. We must adapt to so many changes around us in our global, digital world—demographic, economic, social, and so forth—and take the opportunity to lead our communities. A recent policy brief from the American Library Association's Office for Information Technology Policy, entitled "Confronting the Future: Strategic Visions for the 21st-Century Public Library," articulates a framework for understanding areas where we must be willing to take risks. Roger E. Levien, the policy brief's author, posits four dimensions of strategic decisions that library leaders must make. These dimensions, each viewed on a continuum, are: the physical to virtual libraries, the individual to community libraries, the collection to creation libraries, and the portal to archive library. While the policy brief focuses on public libraries, the four dimensions likely apply as well to other types of libraries. As libraries make and implement decisions about their future directions and services, the actions will have an impact on how those libraries are positioned not just in the short term but also in the medium and long term. How much do we invest in our virtual versus our physical presence, including not just buildings but also physical or virtual resources? How do we address the priorities of individuals while also focusing on the opportunities around serving different segments or our entire community? How do we build our virtual and physical places to serve individuals as well as groups within our communities? What investments should we be making in building our collections, and how can we create opportunities for our library to support knowledge creation, not just knowledge collection? What resource areas are individual libraries uniquely positioned to collect, preserve, and make accessible versus areas where we can provide access to resources hosted elsewhere without consideration of future access?

Library leaders also make strategic decisions that affect what skills and expertise are needed in their employees. Without a willingness to take risks, library leaders may find themselves stuck in a past that does not position them for the opportunities offered in transforming libraries for the future.

COMMUNITY-LED ADVOCACY

Librarians and library communities over the past few decades have grown increasingly aware of the value and impact of community-led advocacy initiatives. Recent successful examples, such as the community-wide effort in Oakland, California, in 2011, included not only widespread testimonials from community members but also media-attracting demonstrations, such as a "zombie crawl," to save half of the branch libraries. The Oakland community members, while receiving support and encouragement from the library they were trying to save, saw ideas and plans originate with different segments of the Oakland community, each speaking to the ways they valued their library.

Community-led library advocacy has power that librarian-led advocacy lacks. With the latter, there is almost always a perceived element of self-interest. On the other hand, we in the library community have witnessed the impact of community members testifying about the value of libraries in their lives. The best way that libraries can contribute to successful community-led advocacy is to help communities identify and then articulate the value proposition of the library. For example, a community may have placed a high value on preparing young children to enter school ready to read. A parent, teacher, or community leader, particularly one who has regular interaction with an elected official or decision maker, with a librarian's collaboration, may be able to find just the right words that resonate with that official's priorities, such as preparing young children to be ready to read.

Library leaders can support these community-led advocacy efforts by collecting and sharing data on the value of libraries in supporting community priorities. Data collection must focus on outcomes from the work the library is doing. In other words, there needs to be a direct connection to the community priorities. Libraries that collect data that does not connect to community priorities will have a very difficult time being valued as essential for the community's advancement.

The library in 2020 can be a critical component for the success of the community it serves. To do so, however, the library not only must transform itself but also must be valued as a leader for the priorities and advancement of its community. The path forward in the coming years is full of challenges and opportunities. The transformation of libraries in a digital, global world brings both excitement and anxiety because decisions made will not only open doors but also close them. Through authentic community engagement, collaboration, inclusion, courageous decisions, and community-led advocacy, libraries in 2020 can be essential to their communities' thriving in the decades to come.

Molly Raphael is immediate past president, American Library Association.

BIBLIOGRAPHY

"Discovering Librarianship: The Future Is Overdue." American Library Association. Web site accessed October 6, 2012. www.ala.org/offices/diversity/imls .

The Harwood Institute for Public Innovation. Web site accessed October 3, 2012. http:// theharwoodinstitute.org .

Levien, Roger E. "Confronting the Future: Strategic Visions for the 21st-Century Public Library." Washington, DC: American Library Association, Office for Information Technology Policy, 2011. http://www.ala.org/offices/oitp/publications/policybriefs.

Save Oakland Libraries. Web site accessed October 6, 2012. www.saveoaklandlibrary.org .

"Spectrum Scholarship Program." American Library Association. Web site accessed October 6, 2012. http://www.ala.org/offices/diversity/spectrum.

Chapter Twelve

Lynn Silipigni Connaway

The library in 2020 will be engagement centered.

In 2008, Lorcan Dempsey stated that it used to be that users built their workflows around the library: resources were scarce, and therefore, the users' attention was abundant. He went on to say that the library now must build its service around the users' workflow because their attention is scarce and the available resources are abundant. This scenario most likely will intensify. As Mitchell Kapor said, "Getting information off the Internet is like taking a drink from a fire hydrant." [1]

The library of the future needs to be constantly changing, or it will not survive. Regardless of whether the library is public or academic, in order to remain relevant in a rapidly changing global environment, it will need to provide an environment for "innovation, productivity, collaboration, and knowledge" (Mathews 2012).

Libraries traditionally have been most concerned with access to information and content (Mathews 2012). Accessing information is no longer an issue. Librarians can fill a niche in the use, creation, and curation of information and content; librarians in 2020 will be assisting users in the creation, evaluation, and production of content. We will not only need to create repositories for content but also to engage and motivate researchers, scholars, and business people to contribute, share, and reuse the content. Librarians will need to develop partnerships with the individuals who create, collect, and analyze data sets in order to provide policies, systems, and services for the storage, access, preservation, and shared use of these data.

Something that often is difficult for library and information professionals to comprehend is that the majority of the population does not use libraries to get information. Many people get their information from human resources (family, teachers, professors, colleagues, peers) and the Internet (Connaway and Dickey 2010; Head and Eisenberg 2010; Prabha, Connaway, and Dickey 2006; Connaway, Lanclos, White, Le Cornu, and Hood 2012; Connaway, White, Lanclos, and Le Cornu 2012). Google and Wikipedia often are the first places individuals go for information regardless of age or educational background (Head and Eisenberg 2010; Head and Eisenberg 2009; Connaway, Lanclos, White, Le Cornu, and Hood 2012; Connaway, White, Lanclos, and Le Cornu 2012). Why? Because people go for what's convenient (Connaway, Dickey, and Radford 2011; Connaway and Dickey 2010).

If this is the case, why not gear library services and systems to those who actually use them? This also may be more efficient for the library. Andy Priestner and Elizabeth Tilley propose this in the concept of boutique academic libraries (Priestner and Tilley 2010 and 2012). They equate the boutique library with the boutique hotel—personalized service. It's a customer-focused approach that will utilize the skills and knowledge of professional librarians, possibly eliminating the more clerical responsibilities of some current library positions. Subject librarians will collaboratively work with users and develop relationships with them to create services specifically geared to their needs.

Relationships are important to both librarians and users. Research in virtual reference services (VRS) reported that both VRS librarians and reference-service users value the relationships developed in both face-to-face (FtF) and virtual environments. Even though VRS is more convenient, users often prefer FtF reference because of the relationships they develop with librarians (Connaway and Radford 2011).

Felicia A. Smith coins the term *helicopter librarians*, based on the concept of helicopter parents. She describes helicopter librarianship as "a holistic approach to a human interaction based on individuality and genuine compassion" (Smith 2012). She stresses the importance of building relationships during instruction sessions and reference encounters and by embracing "new and unconventional methods" for users to contact and interact with librarians when they need help (Smith 2012).

This may call for a new type of librarian and information professional—one who embraces change and possesses a willingness and eagerness to try new technologies and modes of communication and delivery of services. When users visit our online catalogs and websites, they often find them confusing and difficult to use (Connaway and Dickey 2010; Connaway, Prabha, and Dickey 2006). Why not provide a pop-up chat box that asks, "What can I help you find?" We need to be *where* our users need us, *when* they need us. If the majority of our users prefer to communicate via mobile-phone texting, chat, or IM; to learn through gaming; to access the library's unique collections and materials via social media, such as Facebook[2] and Wikipedia; or to meet with us FtF outside of the library, we need to be there!

Today it's not unusual for librarians to make themselves physically available within the academic departments, student unions, and cafeterias, often referred to as embedded librarianship. Kessleman and Watstein state that "bringing the library and the librarian to the user, wherever they are—office, laboratory, home, or even on their mobile device—is at the forefront of what it means to be embedded" (2009, 385). Some academic librarians embed themselves in both FtF and online classes, which provide them with the opportunity to interact with the students and faculty on a regular basis.

A more innovative example of embedded librarianship was the October 2011 announcement that the William H. Welch Medical Library at Johns Hopkins University in Baltimore, Maryland, would close its physical doors to patrons on January 1, 2012.[3] The plan was for the library to continue to provide resources completely online. One of the main reasons for the closing of the library was the decrease in use and circulation of physical materials and the exponential increase in the use of electronic materials. The librarians have been embedded within the academic departments for the past six years and are available to students and faculty via e-mail or phone (Kelley 2011).

Embedded librarianship also is an important aspect of public-library engagement with the community. Many public libraries are providing kiosks in public spaces, such as train and bus stations and parks, for users to check out and return print, audio, and electronic books, magazines, newspapers, and journals.

I was visiting Washington DC several years ago, and as I walked down the street, there were several individuals who were wearing yellow shirts with the word "information" printed on them, standing on the street corners. I decided to ask for directions (although I did not need them). The person was very pleasant, gave me directions, and offered me a map as well. I immediately thought that this would be a perfect venue for public librarians to engage with the community and to communicate the library's value, although I am not necessarily advocating yellow shirts!

A similar idea occurred to me several months ago when a friend, who is very involved in local politics in Aspen, Colorado, called me to discuss the Pitkin County Library's request for funds to renovate and expand the library. Although he had no idea of the library's impact on the community or how the library and its services are used, he felt that the request was unwarranted since the library occupied a beautiful space that was sufficiently staffed and funded to meet the needs of the community. I immediately thought of the information kiosk at the corner of the pedestrian mall in Aspen that is staffed by local volunteers and that I often frequent to find out about daily events, restaurants, and shops. Wouldn't this be the perfect outpost for the library? It would give the library visibility in a bustling small town and would demonstrate the library's engagement with and contributions to the community.

My mother works in retail and always says that "one size fits no one." This pertains to library services and systems as well. No one service or system will meet the needs of every individual. We need to develop an economic model for the allocation of resources for the various modes of user engagement based on the specific user groups' needs and expectations.

The library of 2020 will provide user-centered services and systems that will meet the expectations of the community. The library staff will need to develop relationships with their users and partner with other organizations in order to produce, store, and preserve content and data sets and to provide personalized services. Recruiting and retaining innovative, creative individuals who are willing to engage with users and to embrace new technologies and modes of communication will be imperative for the success of the library of 2020. Access to the library and its resources when and where users need them (which may involve being accessible in multiple physical and virtual locations), will be essential since convenient access to resources, whether human, print, or electronic, is the most critical factor for users. As stated by one of our study participants, "If it is too inconvenient I'm not going after it" (Connaway, Dickey, and Radford 2011). Ultimately, the library must develop strategic plans and continually change and innovate in order to respond proactively instead of reactively to community needs and engagement opportunities.

Lynn Silipigni Connaway is senior research scientist, OCLC Research.

BIBLIOGRAPHY

Connaway, Lynn Silipigni, and Timothy J. Dickey. *The Digital Information Seeker: Report of Findings from Selected OCLC, RIN, and JISC User Behavior Projects.* Bristol: HEFCE, 2010. Web site accessed October 11, 2012. http://www.jisc.ac.uk/media/documents/publications/reports/2010/digitalinformationseekerreport.pdf.
Connaway, Lynn Silipigni, Timothy J. Dickey, and Marie L. Radford. "'If It Is Too Inconvenient I'm Not Going After It:' Convenience as a Critical Factor in Information-Seeking Behaviors." *Library and Information Science Research* 33, no. 3 (2011): 179–90.
Connaway, Lynn Silipigni, Donna Lanclos, David White, Alison Le Cornu, and Erin M. Hood. "User-Centered Decision Making: A New Model for Developing Academic Library Services and Systems." Proceedings from IFLA World Library and Information Congress 2012 Helsinki: "Libraries Now! Inspiring, Surprising, Empowering." http://conference.ifla.org/sites/default/files/papers/wlic2012/76-connaway-en.pdf.
Connaway, Lynn Silipigni, Chandra Prabha, and Timothy J. Dickey. "Phase III: Focus Group Interview Study" of *Sense-Making the Information Confluence: The Whys and Hows of College and University User Satisficing of Information Needs.* Report on National Leadership Grant LG-02-03-0062-03, to Institute of Museum and Library Services, Washington, DC. Columbus: School of Communication, Ohio State University, 2006. Web.
Connaway, Lynn Silipigni, and Marie L. Radford. *Seeking Synchronicity: Revelations and Recommendations for Virtual Reference.* Dublin, OH: OCLC Research, 2011. http://www.oclc.org/reports/synchronicity/full.pdf.

Connaway, Lynn Silipigni, David White, Donna Lanclos, and Alison Le Cornu. "Visitors and Residents: What Motivates Engagement with the Digital Information Environment?" Proceedings from ISIC 2012 Conference, September 5–7, 2012, Tokyo, Japan.

Dempsey, Lorcan. "Always On: Libraries in a World of Permanent Connectivity." *First Monday* 14, no. 1 (2008). Web site accessed October 12, 2012. http://www.firstmonday.org/htbin/cgiwrap/bin/ojs/index.php/fm/article/view/2291/207 .

DeSantis, Nick. "On Facebook, Librarian Brings Two Students from the Early 1900s to Life." *Chronicle of Higher Education*, January 6, 2012. Web site accessed October 12, 2012. http://chronicle.com/blogs/wiredcampus/on-facebook-librarian-brings-two-students-from-the-early-1900s-to-life/34845.

Head, Alison J., and Michael B. Eisenberg. "How Today's College Students Use *Wikipedia* for Course-Related Research." *First Monday* 15, no. 3 (2010). Web site accessed October 11, 2012. http://www.uic.edu/htbin/cgiwrap/bin/ojs/index.php/fm/article/viewArticle/2830/2476.

———. *Lessons Learned: How College Students Seek Information in the Digital Age.* Seattle: The Information School, University of Washington, 2009.

Kelley, Michael. "Major Medical Library Closing Its Doors to Patrons and Moving to Digital Model." *The Digital Shift*, October 27, 2011. Web site accessed October 12, 2012. http://www.thedigitalshift.com/2011/10/research/major-medical-library-closing-its-doors-to-patrons-and-moving-to-digital-model/.

Kesselman, Martin A., and Sarah Barbara Watstein. "Creating Opportunities: Embedded Librarians." *Journal of Library Administration* 49, no. 4 (2009): 383–400.

Mathews, Brian. "Our Strategy: Be Regenerative." The Ubiquitous Librarian. *The Chronicle*, October 4, 2012. Web site accessed October 12, 2012. http://chronicle.com/blognetwork/theubiquitouslibrarian/2012/10/04/our-strategy-be-regenerative/.

———. "Think Like a Startup: A White Paper to Inspire Library Entrepreneurialism." Blacksburg: Virginia Tech University, April 3, 2012. Web site accessed October 11, 2012. http://vtechworks.lib.vt.edu/handle/10919/18649.

Prabha, Chandra, Lynn Silipigni Connaway, and Timothy J. Dickey. "Phase IV: Semi-Structured Interview Study" of *Sense-Making the Information Confluence: The Whys and Hows of College and University User Satisficing of Information Needs.* Report on National Leadership Grant LG-02-03-0062-03, to Institute of Museum and Library Services, Washington, DC. Columbus: School of Communication, Ohio State University, 2006. Web.

Priestner, Andy, and Elizabeth Tilley. "Boutique Libraries at Your Service." *Library and Information Update* 9, no. 6 (2010): 36–39. Web site accessed October 12, 2012. http://personalisedlibraries.files.wordpress.com/2011/01/boutiquelibraries.pdf.

———, eds. *Personalizing Library Services in Higher Education: The Boutique Approach.* Burlington, VT: Ashgate, 2012.

Smith, Felicia A. "Helicopter Librarian: Expect the Unexpected." Backtalk. *Library Journal*, August 28, 2012. Website accessed October 12, 2012. http://lj.libraryjournal.com/2012/08/opinion/backtalk/helicopter-librarian-expect-the-unexpected-backtalk/#_.

NOTES

1. Taken from image: http://www.flickr.com/photos/will-lion/2595497078/; http://giveupinternet.com/2009/01/14/mitchell-kapor-getting-information-off-the-internet-is-like-taking-a-drink-from-a-fire-hydrant-pic/.

2. The director of Research Collections and Services at the University of Nevada, Reno, created Facebook profiles for Joe McDonald, a sophomore at the university in 1913, and his girlfriend and future wife, Leola Lewis, to promote the library's special collections. The profiles have attracted thousands to the special collections (DeSantis 2012).

3. The library did not close its physical doors on January 1, 2012. The board is still reviewing the options to determine which will best provide services to its users.

Chapter Thirteen

Marcellus Turner

The library in 2020 will be, in two words—well, different. I wish I knew more, but I don't. And I guess I should because that is the question I've been asked for the last five years at least, either by library staff, people I meet as I go about my life who ask about my line of work, colleagues who are trying to decide whether they should change careers, and interview teams before they consider extending an offer. Not so surprisingly, my friends and family do not ask the question, and they do not use the library. To put it bluntly, they use me. They use me to research their topics, place items on hold, pick up their items, return their items, and get tickets for authors speaking at a library event. But in the end, no, they do not use the library. But that's family and friends, and "they" are not part of this story because this story is about us— those of us who work in libraries and make them available to our public.

Even though I don't know what libraries will be like exactly, I do know they will be different because we are in a profession that has changed over the years and is still changing. We are being changed by electronic versus print publishing and technology (what information technology can give access to and how it provides access to that information), and the combined change potential is staggering. Changes are occurring right before our very eyes, right in front of us at our reference desks, at our computers, and at our circulation desks. (I wonder if any of these service points will even be around in 2020, or will we meet and serve our customers in a totally different way with a totally different program of service? Hmmm.)

Before I start talking about what libraries will be like, I want to first start with just a bit of reflective history. We've all heard or read about the "Rule of 1965" (Hyman 1999, 54–58). But in case you haven't, the "Rule of 1965" intimates that everything libraries offered before 1965 is basic library service, and therefore, libraries and library staff have traditionally done only three basic things. We check out materials, we answer questions/provide informational assistance, and we offer programming or outreach services. Amazingly, that the work of libraries hasn't changed since 1965 is not much of a surprise. I know that in my twenty-six years in libraries (OK, two years were from waaaayyyy back when I was in fourth and sixth grades and my elementary school required students to work in various offices at the school and I "got" the library) that's all that I've been doing if you don't count cutting out construction-paper leaves and letters for the bulletin board. And that's in a career that spans both academic and public libraries. Yes, we circulate items other than books now, including bicycles, garden tools, smoke detectors; we answer questions in-person, by phone, e-mail, fax, text, chat, and I would imagine Skype somewhere; and we still do outreach and great programming.

Now, I am not contradicting my earlier statement. Libraries *have* changed, yet libraries have stayed the same (maybe that's the sign of a good purpose and mission). What I'm talking about is the "what" of what libraries do, not the "how" of what we do. And it's the "what" that the "Rule of 1965" says hasn't changed.

That's enough on the history of libraries. Now I want to talk about what I think libraries will be like in the future, and 2020 be damned, some of the changes will occur sooner than that. I'm assuming my worthy colleagues who have contributed to this collection of essays will discuss, among other things, reimagined library spaces due to space or flexibility needs; ownership versus access to collections, materials, and resources; library as place— which is not the same as changed library spaces; and the work of MLIS staff. I think these definitely are changes we will see, and they are worthy of reflection and review. I know that my colleagues will do a just job discussing these changes that are being proved already in libraries around the country, so I will leave that to them. I will talk about a few other things, however, that I think are game changers for libraries.

For the record, my first paid library job was in an academic library. I did that for about six years and then switched over to public libraries. So my sharings will be from the public-library perspective. I could posit what will happen with academic libraries, but I'd probably just embarrass myself speaking about things they probably haven't been doing in the last twenty years since I left them. But I will talk about some other things that I think will, in the end, define libraries in the future.

The first and most telling thing that I think will be different is what libraries will offer our customers/patrons/guests. What will we call the people who visit us and use our services in the future? Now that's something I hope will be determined by 2020 even if it's by vote of the customers/ patrons/guests. In 2020, I'm banking on the idea that libraries will be all about offering our guests *experiences*.

It's been said by Jeff Bezos of Amazon (but don't quote me on that because I heard it from somebody who said he said it—maybe) that soon you will be able to acquire anything and everything that you ever want or need online, except for an *experience*. And I see a whole lot of truth and evidence in that. I work online, I shop online, I order food online, and I stay in touch with my non-library-using friends online because it's convenient and relatively easy to do. So when I do something physically, I do it for the experience. That's why I shop at certain stores and frequent certain restaurants. I know what my experience will be. And when I have a bad experience, I try to find another option that is more to my liking and gives me a better experience. That's what libraries will have to do: give great library experiences. Which begs the question, how do we do that?

I think the answer centers on the challenges that libraries are currently facing. I will mention just a few of them, and you will readily see that libraries must give great experiences. Our hours and services have to be more convenient and easy to use, that is, where is the holds area for self-pick up and checkout? We need to review our rules and take some cues from other industries that have great customer-service approaches like Nordstrom and Starbucks. We need to make sure our technology and websites rival that which our patrons are using at home without the wonkiness. And we've got to be more externally focused and less internally focused (just for whose convenience are we scheduling that genealogy class anyway?). If we can do those things, we can give great experiences. Overall, I think that will be our most defining moment.

The next thing that I think will be different about libraries is the specialization or customizable connection of our program of service to our communities. A public library's program of service tends to center on service to the general interests of the user population. This means that programming and outreach is designed for the residents of that city or neighborhood. The collection is built around the interests and education levels of the users. If a library chooses to move away from that and focus on something else, say, its city history (not that they shouldn't be doing that anyway), then some appeal to the general audience might be lost. Truthfully, I think it's fair for library systems to customize their offerings based on the needs of their communities. That is the only way they will stay relevant and of value, and lest you think otherwise, libraries *must* remain relevant and of value to survive in 2020. So, by system or by city or by neighborhood, libraries in 2020 may specialize for a different purpose or audience and, thereby, differ from their neighbor, or from what they used to be. And that might make for the biggest divergence for libraries as a collective.

The third thing that I think will be different is our employees. I can say that because the work will change, and when the work changes, organizational needs change, thus, qualifications of the employees change. There will be at least two reasons for changes in our staffing. The first change centers on current staffing and work. As we are already noticing, the number of physical items that we work with and move is decreasing. Our customers may not have clearly spoken, but they are mumbling louder, and they are telling us they like the ease and convenience of reading on electronic devices, if not just fiddling with them. In that sense, some of the work we currently perform in the library will decrease just because we will not move the same amounts of materials as in the past. Don't panic, however. We still have many fans and lovers of the physical book, and trust me, they mumble and grumble just as loud as our electronic users, and we haven't reached a tipping point yet. But we need to be prepared, and realigning staff and the work they perform is the start.

Likewise, many of our patrons are doing their own research and getting "close enough" because "close enough" is all they need. This means that our informational-assistance services will change. We will have to figure out how to connect with our customers and assist them when "close enough" isn't enough.

In the end, many of our staff will have new duties because there is less of their current work and more opportunity to do some other work or a combination thereof.

I envision the second staffing change a bit differently. As I mentioned earlier, some of the change that will occur in libraries will be related to the program of service a library may choose to offer. If the program of service foregoes the general interests of the population or specializes to any degree to meet the interests/demands of another population (yes, both could easily happen and could/should probably coexist), then workers from other professions have a great opportunity to work in libraries. For example, libraries that focus on early-childhood education might employ educators, academicians, or teachers to help us with research into early-childhood learning or teaching, to some degree. Focusing more on outreach might mean we need project managers or community leaders who have connections that library staff may not have. And what about writing programs? Why not employ a writer-in-residence or a journalist/reporter to lead the series or help us with teens who want to write or interact with local authors who are learning to navigate publishing or self-publishing. We might even find a publisher or newspaper editor looking for work (oops, I mean additional work). Reader's advisory? What about using social-media-savvy bloggers with great followings to help us push our collections in the virtual world?

Librarianship is a calling to service. Those who work in libraries and fully commit to working in them over time do so for the service aspect. Workers from other professions have this same service calling and could find fulfillment working in the library of 2020.

All in all, I think these three measures will be our greatest game changers. They will be what define or redefine libraries. So, to paraphrase an old adage, I may not know libraries, but I know them when I see them. And I'm looking forward to seeing them.

For as long as libraries have been around and with as many years as I've spent working in them and adapting to the changes that come along, I'm fairly certain that libraries will be here in 2020. Maybe a bit different from what they are now and maybe a lot different from what I envision—hey, we're all pretty much guessing right now anyway. But the business that we are in and our purpose—providing access to information—will not have changed. Libraries in 2020 will still serve as the citizen's personal ladder for upward growth, knowledge, and insight. And since that won't change, then we still have opportunities for library work and library staff—traditional and new. Long live the "Rule of 1965."

Marcellus Turner is city librarian of the Seattle Public Library.

BIBLIOGRAPHY

Hyman, Karen. "Customer Service and the 'Rule of 1965.'" *American Libraries*, October 1999: 54–58.

Chapter Fourteen

Ruth Faklis

The library in 2020 will be . . . better than ever.

In my opinion, the essence of libraries in 2020 will be better than ever. Why the qualification of "essence"? Because economic reality will take its toll on all types of libraries as we know them today, and the role of the librarian will continue to be besieged by society. Allow me to explain.

I am a thirty-seven-year veteran of library services in Illinois, including elementary and high school, corporate, and public library experience. This multi-type knowledge has given me a uniquely positive—yet jaded—look at the future of libraries. Let us examine the issues one by one and in no particular order.

Economy: There are a number of libraries in financial trouble right now. Municipal governments are cutting library budgets to provide for life-safety (police/fire) expenses, coverage of pension promises, or infrastructure up-keep. Property-tax-based libraries are being fiscally hurt by the mass number of foreclosures.

Technology: It seems like each new day brings a new technological gadget that allows access to worldwide information. These items are for sale to the general public, and their costs are becoming minimal. Their features include wireless technology in smaller than pocket-sized cases. Indeed, some schools issue computers with textbooks already downloaded for individual student study. The evolution of technology in the next decade should provide for even more amazing packaged offerings.

Society: Every time I read an issue of American Library Association's *Library Hotline*, it never ceases to amaze me at just what public libraries are looked upon to provide. This includes, but is not limited to, keepers of the homeless and registered sex offenders while simultaneously offering latch-key children a safe and activity-filled haven. We have been asked to be voter-registration sites, warming stations, notaries, technology-terrorism watch-dogs, senior social-gathering centers, election sites, substitute sitters during teacher strikes, and the latest—postmasters. These requests of society are ever evolving. Funding is not generally attached to these magnanimous sug-gestions, and when it is, it does not cover actual costs of the additional burden, thus stretching the library's budget even further. I know of no other government entity that is asked to take on additional responsibilities not necessarily aligned with its mission.

Gangs: School and public libraries have established close ties with local police authorities in the war on gangs. Librarians and staff members are educated on gang signs, colors, and habits. They are trained on how best to defuse a situation involving weapons, violence, and customer safety. Many neighborhoods—including mine—have experienced gang drive-bys involv-ing random gunfire, yet within hours of the shoot-out have hosted outdoor summer-reading celebrations with hundreds of participants.

Facilities: When a new library can be erected, it is cause for celebration. Many existing libraries, such as my own, have undergone three to four reno-vations for additional floor space, technology needs, specialized program-ming rooms, silent study areas, and the like. These efforts require constant maintenance on unbalanced air and heating units, deteriorating roofs, build-ing-stress cracks, rotting window frames, electrical overloads, sprinkler-sys-tem requirements, and ADA (Americans with Disabilities Act) needs.

Librarianship/Information Technologist: My suggestion is if you are in library school right now—wake up—you've got a wild ride in front of you. While the class work involves an understanding of reference skills, administra-tion needs, technology trends, fiscal understanding, collection develop-ment, and classification of materials, these are basic requirements of the job in a field that requires ongoing continuing education. Just as a doctor or lawyer must keep abreast of new medical breakthroughs or the passage of new laws, librarians must also renew their understanding of library laws, financial effects, media types, technology offerings, staff policies, and cus-tomer issues.

Health and Safety: Multi-type libraries house defibrillators and train staff in their use as well as in resuscitation and stroke identification. In a medical emergency, schools have the luxury of knowing the student's name and his or her medical history and perhaps even house a school nurse. Other types of librarians must be trained to react to a medical emergency in the best interest of the victim as well as the multi-aged customers witnessing the event.

Weather: In the case of a weather emergency, such as a tornado warning, the librarian must be trained in staying calm and directing the customers to a predetermined safe space within the facility. In a school or public library, librarians may actually be asked to tell stories to calm the youngsters in their charge during the waiting period. They also must be firm in informing the public that each person is required to follow library emergency procedures or leave the building, so as not to jeopardize the safety the whole.

Fire: It is a similar case in a fire emergency. If an alarm is pulled, the librarian and staff must remain calm as they lead the students or customers to a predetermined meeting site, leaving no one behind. Although it may be difficult to know how many patrons were using the facility at the time, it is suggested that the library keep a daily roster of employees who are actually in the building so they may be retrieved by firemen if necessary.

Advocacy: It behooves librarians not only to keep abreast of federal, state, and local legislation that may affect their service initiatives but also to initiate any legislation they determine is in the best interest of their type library or customer needs. I highly suggest that librarians of like interests meet on a regular basis and discern common desires. I further suggest that librarians continue to actively pursue their local legislators and promote their libraries and the services offered. It is important to be proactive, not reactive, on issues that may affect any aspect of library service.

After all I have iterated, how do I come to the conclusion that "the library in 2020 will be . . . better than ever"?

The centuries have witnessed the evolution of libraries and their importance and resiliency to the societies they served. The common thread over the years is that libraries have stored and preserved history and knowledge. Tales of the libraries from those created by the Sumerians in southern Mesopotamia, the Assyrians in northern Mesopotamia, and Egyptians in Alexandria are as well known and documented as those created by Aristotle, Benjamin Franklin, and Andrew Carnegie. In ancient times, records were stored on a variety of materials, such as papyrus, parchment, wood, and clay. Today, we too store our information in a variety of formats, such as acid-free paper, CDs, DVDs, and flash drives. Again, the types of storage in which we preserve the history have evolved, and this in turn will allow us to shed traditional public neighborhood, local school, corporate, and even academic facilities. In their stead, we will use handheld technology and keep "hub" libraries for traditional library services. These hub libraries will be financially underwritten by many communities joining together, whether on the level of public, school, academic, or corporate library. The traditional facility will be centrally located to all underwriting its costs and house librarians who are educated in library science and continue to grow techno-savvy in service to their customers. Whether all this absolutely takes place by 2020, I cannot foresee, but I do accept that we've already started the journey to that end.

It is my belief that the most dramatic, dare I say drastic, change will be in the role of librarian. I highly doubt that the librarians in ancient Ephesus were forced by society to be more than a keeper, even retriever, of information. I truly cannot envision them being entrusted to oversee latchkey youngsters as their parents worked in the marketplace. The future librarians will finally, and most happily, be forced out of the "bun and sensible shoes" image and catapulted into the "keeper of all knowledge with a finger on the trigger of technology" image. Users will depend on them to continue to monitor and review data sites for accuracy and currency of information. The all-important issue of determining the customer's actual question or need will still be in the skill set of the information librarian. But in the future, it may not be necessary for all librarians to be physically located at the hub locations. They very well may be able to work in the comfort of their homes or as easily on a warm, sandy, tropical beach. As long as they can retrieve the question and access the information via modernized technology, librarians will be able to work from most locations around the globe. Their essential networking and continuing-education efforts may also be accomplished via modernized technology.

Specifically regarding the economic reality of library service, I foresee libraries using the Illinois Park District model. They will no longer rely solely on the whim or will of municipal authorities nor the unstable property or sales tax revenues. These types of funds may continue to underwrite the basic operations expenses of the hub library, but by 2020, I predict that libraries will collect an additional surcharge for story-time programs, author venues, craft creations, after-school programs, and the like. I envision that the user's library card will no longer be limited to an area of service but rather be totally universal in scope. As long as they pay the surcharge, their quest for information or service will be offered in any location. Therefore, I predict a more active, modern, constantly evolving library in 2020, one that will be better than ever.

Ruth Faklis is director, Prairie Trails Public Library District.

Chapter Fifteen

Susan Hildreth

The library in 2020 will be the vibrant hub of its community. In developing the strategic plan for the Institute of Museum and Library Services (IMLS), "Creating a Nation of Learners 2012–2016," the vision of a viable and vibrant future for libraries was a key priority. Libraries are changing and will continue to do so as their communities diversify and grow. But there will always be several domains where libraries are uniquely positioned to provide crucial value to their communities: they provide opportunities for all types of learning experiences, they are community anchors, and they serve as platforms for the creation and preservation of all types of content, while also providing public access to content. By focusing on these key areas of activity and investment, each the subject of a goal in the IMLS strategic plan, libraries will ensure their relevancy and vibrancy in 2020 and beyond.

The library in 2020 must be considered as part of the educational ecosystem of its community. It is the institution best positioned to provide lifelong learning for all ages. Informal and out-of-school learning will become increasingly important as many educational programs are delivered virtually. The library can be a source of virtual learning, but it is uniquely positioned to provide free gathering spaces for all types of learning activities and learners. The library can provide the actual learning experience or make the connection between those who have learning needs and interests and those who can provide it.

Libraries have always been involved in meeting the learning needs of children aged zero–five years. As the cruciality of these early learning experiences becomes even more evident through recent brain research, the role of the library in this area becomes essential. Working with infants to toddlers to pre-kindergarten can provide huge benefits to the new learners, their parents and caregivers, and their communities. The library can actually bring these audiences together and provide these services at the facility. It may be more effective to provide these services outside of the library in the community. Finally, the library may serve as the connector that facilitates external experts working with these audiences, either within or outside of the library. In any case, the library plays a key role in early learning success.

Twenty-first-century skills, crucial to learning success, are characterized by the "four Cs": creativity, collaboration, communication, and critical thinking. These skills are needed to succeed today and will remain in high demand in 2020. They are not based on knowledge of specific content; they are the abilities needed to analyze and solve problems regardless of the content area. Content knowledge remains important, but critical thinking skills are essential for success in a world where content is constantly changing and evolving. The library in 2020 will be one of the primary locations for understanding and obtaining these critical skills.

Digital media has become part of our life and is changing rapidly. Skills required for effective use of digital media are very much in alignment with twenty-first-century skills. Although people of all ages have an interest in it, young adults are especially comfortable with using media to tell their story. IMLS and the MacArthur Foundation are funding digital-media labs based on the model of the YOUMedia space at the Chicago Public Library. Although teens learn skills at these labs that may lead to careers, the most impactful outcome is the relationship that develops between the teen and the mentor who supports the teen in the learning process. Effective mentors strengthening the lives of teens in digital media labs and other library environments will be widespread in 2020.

Twenty-first-century-skills acquisition can be jump-started by getting our hands dirty and creating things out of a wide variety of materials. Challenging and fun for all ages, these learning experiences are becoming available in "makers' spaces" that are being created in libraries all over the world. From using a 3-D printer to creating objects from wire and old PC parts, maker labs are the community-learning venues of the twenty-first century and will be coming to a library near you.

Each community has its own demographics that must be considered in service planning, but we know that by 2020, 22 percent of the population will be over sixty, the "boomer generation." The successful library in 2020 will have a service plan to meet the needs of this significant target audience. Most boomers see themselves as active learners with discretionary time and a wide variety of interests. They are accustomed to services tailored to their individual needs, and this service approach must be adopted to effectively serve them. Although customized service can be a challenge for libraries, it will be critical for successful customer engagement in 2020. Also, boomers are accustomed to being in charge and may desire a significant role in developing or managing library services. This interest is one that libraries need to embrace since the boomers can become a key support group and add significantly to a library's service capacity.

The specific term "community anchor" is taken from the National Broadband Plan, and it may be modified by 2020, but the service it describes is critical and one that libraries have been fulfilling for many years.

The critical role libraries have played in providing access to public computers and to high-speed broadband has been well documented. Particularly for rural and low-income urban neighborhoods, this has been a lifeline for the community. Access to job information, health information, financial literacy, and communication with far-flung family members has brought immeasurable value to users. Although computers are pervasive in our society and much communication has moved to mobile devices, there are still over 100 million people, one-third of the U.S. population, who are not digitally literate. The Federal Communications Commission has recently created a national initiative, Connect to Compete (C2C), to address this literacy gap. C2C will launch a national advertising campaign in early 2013 to drive people to digital literacy services, with a particular emphasis on libraries as providers. Libraries already serve as the nation's de facto digital literacy corps. By 2020, there will certainly be another technological innovation creating a new skills gap, so it is critical that the library continue to provide access to the latest technology and skills training so everyone can have a chance to succeed.

Libraries are serving as portals for many public services, and that role will continue to expand as funding limitations impact in-person customer-service options and more public services are provided exclusively online. Many libraries work with their local workforce boards to serve as career centers. Some libraries provide passport services, marriage licenses, voter registration, and local government services. The library assumed widespread responsibility from the United States Postal Service (USPS) for distributing income tax forms. Now the USPS is calling upon libraries to serve as "village post offices" in communities that may lose their local postal service, particularly in rural areas. Although the community-service priorities in 2020 may vary from those of today, libraries must be proactive in identifying those priorities and be as flexible as possible in cooperating with a wide variety of partners in providing those services.

How can the library effectively identify these community needs? By embracing its role in civic engagement. Again, the library is uniquely positioned to serve as the community convener in identifying local challenges and bringing together the participants to address them. The library is a trusted, neutral institution with easy access to information that can address community issues. The library can provide the physical space and a safe environment for dialogue on potentially contentious issues. This is a role that libraries must take on purposefully as it will require library staff to become skilled in facilitating challenging conversations. In an era when civil dialogue is fast disappearing, it is critical that libraries move into the civic-engagement space. More than any other institution, libraries have the potential for success in this special niche.

Preserving, analyzing, and providing access to content are the hallmark roles of library services, and creation of content is a critical task in the twenty-first century. In 2020, the role of the library as an open-content platform will be embedded in all services provided and all interactions with users. Although practically all libraries have websites, the most visited section of those websites is the catalog. The catalog will take on the role of one-stop shopping center for content. People are eager to look for specific content and want to have choices in how they access that content. Choice of format, availability status, the option of a reserve list, and quick access to purchase will be readily available options through the catalog. Using the library catalog as a channel for purchases from publishers will address, at least to some extent, publishers' concerns regarding the viability of their distribution models. Also, print-on-demand stations will be available extensively so requests for materials that are not housed on-site or readily available electronically can be easily provided.

Libraries will provide personalized service to all patrons. Recommendations tailored to personal interests or based on reading or listening history will be readily available. The individualized service that has become the norm in the private sector will be provided in the public sector as well. But the library will always maintain confidentiality of personal information if requested.

The library platform will also be used for content creation. Libraries will continue to create space for conversations about all kinds of topics, including what we read, listen to, experience, and so forth. Imagine a community where the librarian serves as the connector for an individual who needs highly specialized information. The librarian can start the conversation with library resources and also connect the individual through the library platform to a community of experts on the topic. Libraries will provide virtual space for individual content creation that can be shared, curated, edited, and made available for many uses. The library can highlight its unique niche in preserving local history by supporting the documentation of local activities, for example, school plays or local festivals archived on the library website.

The world of local print journalism has dramatically shifted, and community journalism will be widespread by 2020. The library will be a partner in this space by supporting local news activities in a number of ways. The library platform may become the virtual home for all local information sharing. Local journalism activities may be housed at the library. The support of community journalism is a component of both the content and community-anchor goals outlined in the IMLS strategic plan.

More open, transparent government at all levels is a requirement in twenty-first-century society. The library will play an important role in supporting this transparency by providing free and open access to government information from the local to federal level. This dovetails with community-journalism support because providing access to government information is critical for a well-informed democracy. Access to information is valuable, but its value is significantly increased when community journalism sets the information in the unique context of the local community.

In a world where the same information is available to everyone at a moment's notice, the library in 2020 will add significant value by focusing on unique, local information that is not found in any other source. Providing opportunities for the public to access and enhance this unique content will enrich knowledge and position the library as the key contributor to the life of the community. The preservation of this unique local content, no matter what the format, is a critical role that the library is well suited to fulfill. But even more important than preservation is the opportunity that the library platform can provide for content creation by both the library staff and public. The ability to create, share, and preserve locally developed content will be one of the highly valued services of the twenty-first-century library.

As libraries adapt to the needs of their communities, the shift of collections from print to digital must be considered. The actual physical space that will be needed to house print collections in 2020 will be significantly reduced from what is currently needed and used. Print materials may be digitized with print copies in regional depositories, stored in compact shelving in off-site or low-cost spaces, or available by print-on-demand services. No matter what the disposition of print materials looks like, this shift will create physical space that can be allocated for new and different uses in libraries. It is important for libraries to engage with their communities right now in order to determine the highest priorities for this newly available space. Libraries, beloved by the public, represent a significant built inventory of public space that should be retained for civic or public purposes, including support for economic development. Siting business incubators and fully outfitted office environments in libraries are examples. There may even be some commercial uses of space that would be beneficial to the community, but planners should be proactive, ensuring that the public good remains paramount.

I am confident that in 2020 the library will be the vibrant hub of its community, providing the services and opportunities I have described here. To realize that vision, however, each library must work in partnership with the community to identify the services that achieve the greatest public good. Focusing on these services, which may vary greatly across the country, will result in a strong library making its community even stronger.

Susan Hildreth is director of the Institute of Museum and Library Services.

IV

Place

Chapter Sixteen

Stacey A. Aldrich and Jarrid P. Keller

The library in 2020 will be everywhere and somewhere.

The future is already here, it is just unevenly distributed .
—William Gibson

When we began to think about writing a piece about the future of libraries, we thought it might be interesting to approach the future from the types of jobs that might be in libraries in the next ten years. We based our future descriptions on the following trends: (1) information everywhere, (2) continuing increase in use of mobile and embedded technology, (3) rise of social knowledge, (4) longer living and the emergence of lifestyle design, and (5) integration of robotics into the world. We invite you to join Phyllis, the human-connection expert, as she reviews five job descriptions. As you read with Phyllis, what picture of the library forms in your mind from just the job descriptions? What assumptions are being made about the future? Do you already kind of do some of this work? What is the same? What is different?

Phyllis is the new human-connection expert for northern California. She is responsible for mapping the needs of each the communities to the right people. Her biggest challenge these days is balancing the robotic and human elements of staffing and services to the public. This morning, Phyllis met with a library director to go over some of the latest job descriptions for four positions that need to be filled. As Phyllis begins to review the job descriptions, she is amused how similar but different they are from just ten years ago. The libraries are everywhere, and they are also public places.

Position Title: Embedded librarian.

Importance of Position: The embedded librarian is responsible for physically and virtually traveling around all communities to catalog all pieces of the environment to be added to the Global Brain Library (GBL). This position is vital for ensuring that all people can use their embedded or wearable technology to get instant information about everything that is in their surroundings. This position also provides network and information assistance to the public while in the field collecting information.

Projects: The first year of this position will focus on three areas: (1) trees in historic parks, (2) monuments, and (3) government buildings. This position will be expected to identify other gaps in the Global Brain Library for future cataloging.

Skills: This position requires the ability to:

work outside and in an open environment and remotely with colleagues
work virtually in 3-D environment using avatar to engage colleagues
communicate effectively with people to gather information and appropriate images
use the latest hardware and software for the GBL
implement the latest GBL cataloging and metadata standards
provide network and information assistance to the public
be flexible and continuously learn, unlearn, and relearn

Position Title: Content packaging librarian

Importance of Position: The content packaging librarian is responsible for making dynamic connections among library and community information so that users can easily find information that relates to particular topics and can also lead them to other beneficial information.

Projects: The first year of this position will focus on building social knowledge by packaging community information and creating processes for farming all information in all formats as it relates to governmental meetings. This is a new area and will require close work with the Global Brain Library (GBL).

Skills: This position requires the ability to:

use all formats of information including physical and digital
communicate effectively with all stakeholders and obtain appropriate permissions for using all information
make dynamic connections among all kinds of information as it relates to a topic
use the latest GBL cataloging and metadata standards
obtain feedback from users to determine if content packages are complete
recruit and coordinate content-packaging community volunteers
be flexible and continuously learn, unlearn, and relearn

Title: Robotic maintenance engineer

Importance of Position: The robotic maintenance engineer is responsible for ensuring that all public-assistant and stack robots are in good working order to support the needs of the public. The public assistant robots must have the latest syntax and 3-D holographic avatar software to be able to help patrons in the library. The stack robots must be able to find and retrieve materials to provide to patrons upon request.

Projects: The first year of this position will be responsible for daily maintenance and support of all robots and will be required to examine the current models and software to create a draft plan for future upgrades and management.

Skills: This position requires the ability to:

manage the hardware and software of first-generation public-assistant and
    stack robots
communicate effectively with staff and patrons
evaluate and create project plans
manage and train staff working with robots
be flexible and continuously learn, unlearn, and relearn

Position Title: Lifestyle design librarian

Importance of Position: The lifestyle design librarian is responsible for leading a team of librarians who specialize in individualized and customized assistance for public members navigating learning, career transitions, health, and any other specific needs. This position provides the human touch to help connect people to the exact resources needed to be successful.

Projects: The first year of this position will focus on the systems of delivery of service to the public. Recent surveys indicate that patrons would like more physical meetings to begin their lifestyle design plans. This position will also work with the World Education Network to facilitate connections to personal education plans and build blended-learning opportunities for the community to meet at the library for human connection.

1. *Skills*: This position requires the ability to:

facilitate and lead a dynamic team of lifestyle design staff
communicate effectively with multiple stakeholders
create supportive communication with patrons
evaluate services and provide continuous improvement
be flexible and continuously learn, unlearn, and relearn

Position Title: Global Brain Library (GBL) cloud engineer

Importance of Position: The GBL cloud engineer is responsible for providing system requirements for the development of Application Protocol Interface (API) Web-service protocols, which allow the GBL to interface with other cloud-based brain library's data warehouses worldwide, increasing capacity and accessibility of information for the public.

Projects: The first year of this position will require the GBL cloud engineer to define API Web-service requirements based on the GBL's collection. This will ensure successful interface and exchange of cloud-based data, including geo-coding all library datasets for easier discovery and correlation of data to better serve the needs of the public.

Skills: This position requires the ability to:

understand API Web services and geo-coding standards
extensive knowledge of GPL cloud holdings
communicate effectively with all stakeholders and obtain appropriate permissions for using all information
use the latest GBL cataloging and metadata standards
be flexible and continuously learn, unlearn, and relearn

Phyllis was comfortable with these job descriptions and felt confident that she knew someone who would be perfect for the robotic maintenance engineer. She knew someone who had started out as a librarian and then added robotic care to his skillset. The other positions she would create info for the Jobstream and other channels.

Before you read the job descriptions, we invited you to consider a few questions. We would love hear what picture of the future was created in your mind. We'd also like to hear what other future jobs you think are going to be in libraries in the future. Please send your thoughts to stacey.aldrich@gmail.com or tweet with hashtag #futurelibjobs.

P.S. Stacey wants to be a lifestyle design librarian and Jarrid wants to be a robotic maintenance engineer.

Stacey A. Aldrich is deputy secretary, Pennsylvania Department of Education, Office of Commonwealth Libraries.

Jarrid P. Keller is acting deputy state librarian of California.

Chapter Seventeen

John Dove

The library in 2020 will be dispersed and ubiquitous. Access to information from anywhere at any time without speed bumps will be the norm. But to meet the inherent needs of users, librarians at libraries of all types will need to take on a new focus on obtaining and tuning effective information filters rather than just focusing on what content to provide. The key questions about users are: what are their needs, and what barriers can we eliminate so that they can fulfill these needs?

I remember a particular study I first learned of from Joe Janes's *Introduction to Reference Work in the Digital Age* (2003) about a company that, back in 2000, engaged a marketing firm to study the information needs of a cross section of the public. In this study, 74 people were asked to carry a recording device so that at any time during the day they could record any question to which they wished they could have an immediate answer. After four days of recording, the participants were each interviewed and asked how much they would have gladly paid for answers to their questions if these answers could be provided for them on the spot. The researchers then extrapolated this value of unanswered questions and determined that in the U.S. adult population alone there were $150 billion worth of unanswered questions per year waiting there for the right company to come along and provide the answers. One of the remarkable things about this study was the reported average number of questions people had each day; it was just over four. Personally, I have more than four questions each morning even before I've put on my shoes, including "Where in the world did I put my shoes last night?"

You might guess that the company sponsoring this study was Google, but no, it was a company building a website based on astrology. I guess they figured that they had a source for all unanswered questions and now just needed a way to monetize that source of all answers. Makes you wonder why they needed to do a marketing study![1]

Google itself has certainly gone a long way toward meeting the informational needs revealed by this study. The speed at which we are experiencing improvements in ubiquitous access to useful information is truly astonishing. I've always been one to try out things before others just to see if it could be done. Shortly after I joined Xrefer in late 2003, I figured out how to connect my Palm Treo to Xreferplus (now Credo Reference). It required a bit of persistence and patience to get the connection that year to work without speed bumps. But I was able to do then what is now quite commonplace. I remember shortly thereafter going to the movies with my wife to see *Mona Lisa Smile*, in which Julia Roberts plays a West Coast college professor in the early 1950s trying to make her way into the East Coast culture of Wellesley College (Newell 2003). In a scene in which she and a new friend among the professors are watching as people file into the assembly hall, her new professor friend is explaining why Wellesley is different from any university she'd have been familiar with in California. He points out a couple coming into the hall and says, "See that couple? They are the Joneses. They are the very Joneses for which the expression 'keeping up with the Joneses' came from." A few seconds later, after consulting Xreferplus via my Treo, I elbowed my wife and whispered, "It's not true." "What's not true?" "That comment about the Joneses. According to the *American Heritage Dictionary of Idioms*, the expression 'keeping up with the Jones' was first coined in 1913 by a cartoonist named Arthur R. Momand. That couple could not have been the origin of that expression" (*The American Heritage Dictionary of Idioms* 1997). "Oh Shush!" said my wife.

Have you noticed the changes in everyday life regarding access to information? What car of families, college students, or coworkers doesn't navigate along the highway without someone on a smartphone, using it not only as a set of yellow pages overlaid on satellite images, road maps, and Yelp reviews but also sources to answer questions coming up in conversation, like "Who won the gold medal in the 100 meters at Athens in 2000?" "When will the moon rise tonight?" "Who starred in that movie about bicycles at Indiana University?"

I'm now no longer surprised when speaking with either of my adult sons over the phone when any claim, large or small, that I make about the world is quickly being challenged by a son double tasking his call from Dad by pointing and clicking around Google, the Internet, and Wikipedia. For example, I was recently on Skype with my son in Slovakia and mentioned an inexpensive Italian and Chinese restaurant, the China Roma, that had newly opened a branch of their restaurant on Revere Beach where my wife and I live. They were featuring a dish I'd never heard of before, a "chop suey sandwich." Without even a momentary pause, he replied that the chop suey sandwich was a local specialty of the North East suburbs of Boston and still served by only two restaurants in the area. This all came from Wikipedia. Since the Wikipedia entry didn't mention the China Roma, you can be sure that the Wikipedia entry was updated within 10 minutes after our phone conversation.[2]

We all have similar experiences of the vast changes in the flow of information in recent years. With such rapid shifts underway, how can we begin to predict what 2020 will be like? Personally, I find it most useful to look to the past when trying to predict the future. That way you can look at fundamentals without the noise of the current applications of those principles. It allows one to look at a question from the standpoint of *general systems thinking*, as the term is used by Gerald Weinberg's book of that name (Weinberg 1975). A general systems thinker is the kind of person who arrives in Bangkok and remarks how Bangkok reminds him of Pittsburgh because they are both cities.

For questions about the history of reference content, I often turn to Tom McArthur's *Worlds of Reference*. It illuminates the connections between the past and the future. His history of reference over a two-thousand-year period is able to achieve a long view that enables us to examine the future from the vantage point of 1988 without being distracted by the popularity of passing fads like Second Life.

Countless experts have pointed out how an acceleration of content creation has led to information overload in almost every field of endeavor. Clay Shirky famously pointed out in a talk at the Web 2.0 conference in NYC in 2008 that the problem is not one of information overload but one of "filter failure."[3] We don't have in place the best filters that could bring into our view what's important to us and leave all the remainder out of view. He asserts that this problem has been with us ever since Gutenberg; the printing press exploded the available information one could find or refer to. Ann Blair, professor of history at Harvard University, in her recently published book, *Too Much to Know: Managing Scholarly Information before the Modern Age* (2010), examines reference works, many of which predate Gutenberg, to show how essential they were in helping people more quickly gain mastery of the contributions of the great thinkers. Each of these reference works and their finding aides were, in a sense, effective filters, and many of these reference works were developed before Gutenberg.

The main point of this is that the anthropologic need for well-crafted filters has thousands of years of history, and we are nowhere near the end of what today's technologies could provide. Smartphones, Google, the Open Web, GPS data, and Wikipedia have done a lot to make relevant, desirable information dispersed and ubiquitous, but there are a lot of contexts in which we as lifelong learners still experience speed bumps (or lockouts), on the one hand, and information overload on the other. There is a lot of work yet to do to bring the ease of use we now experience searching for restaurants and bus schedules to the world of learning. A lot of that work will emerge in the next ten years.

One way to put succinctly the objectives of the new reference and searching tools ("filters" in Clay Shirkey's sense of the word) is to look back to Margaret Hutchins, who wrote the leading textbook for training reference librarians back in the 1940s. After discussing all of the features of reference works, reference rooms, reference desks, and particularly reference librarians, she boils it all down to say that effective reference work "saves the time of busy people" (Hutchins 1944, 206).

Applying that phrase to today's and tomorrow's world, we quickly realize that all of us are "busy" in different ways. Google ads and the customization that many websites already do to select what we each are individually most likely to want to buy or search for has shown how valuable such customization can be but is limited to the Open Web world and misses some key aspects of our individual contexts.

Our "busy-ness" is characterized by a context that includes not just our daily life and shopping needs but also the institutions and communities that we participate in. For instance, a student's "busy-ness" is greatly influenced by the goals and objectives the student has to achieve in order to get to a standard of learning that is characterized by a particular course of study in a particular institution. Employees in companies are expected these days not only to have certified levels of skills to do one job but also to continue as lifelong learners and gain additional skills, some of which are specific to that particular company. And there are many reasons why we as citizens and perpetual learners will continue to turn to public libraries to give us access to information that is particular to our interests and communities.

My principal prediction about libraries in 2020 is that they will pay greater attention to the provision of individually and institutionally specific filters that empower learners to focus on what is most useful to them in the current multidimensional contexts of their lives. To meet Margaret Hutchins's goal of saving "the time of busy people," these filters will need to jump firewalls, eliminate speed bumps, and capture the goals and missions of institutions to which people belong.

I'll mention briefly a glimpse into this possible future via two examples of new library technologies: the personalized ranking recently introduced into Ex Libris's Web-scale discovery tool, Primo, with its Central Index, and Topic Pages from Credo Reference. Personalized ranking in Primo, version 4, allows users to opt in to providing a user profile, which will then effect the ranking of results from Primo's vast search of the holdings of the user's library. For example, if a user searches for information about "normalization," Primo can recognize through the user's profile that this student is a computer-science major and thus can provide results that pertain to database design at a higher rank than the very different uses of that term in political science or psychology. The reason I say that this is just a glimpse into the future is that as soon as you start down the path of thinking about how to make effective academic filters, you quickly realize that the filtering of students' academic interests present many interesting opportunities for enhancing this personalized ranking even further. It's not uncommon that the graduate-level departments at large universities will have a focus that would be distracting to the undergraduate student who is just starting out with his or her 101-level course work. And most students at the 101 level are taking courses in multiple subjects, so they can't count on a ranking of results that only focuses on one subject. Interdisciplinary subjects (which often are where new insights surface) are rife with conflicting uses of terminologies.

Topic Pages from Credo Reference have two essential characteristics that relate to the design of effective filtering. First is the fact that they reside on the Open Web. Secondly, they are presented to the user in a way that merges institutionally specific results crafted by the librarians of that institution in order to lead the user to the best resources for going deeper into that particular search. So this combines the dual aspects of the future I see: access from anywhere without speed bumps combined with institutionally specific filtering into the most promising places to go next. Currently, a student at NYU and a student at Columbia coming upon the same Credo Topic Page via a Google search will see a different rendition of a Credo Topic Page because portions of that page have been tailored by algorithms tuned by different librarians at each university. They'll both get a general explanation of the search term or phrase from a reliable source, but along with that, they will see results from the best databases and resources that the librarians at NYU and Columbia think a student researching that topic should consider for deeper explanations. The reason I say this, too, is just a glimpse is that much needs to be done to allow such Topic Pages to be tuned to the specific academic level of the student doing the searching.

One could easily imagine effective filtering that combines some of the aspects of Primo's personalized ranking and Credo's jumping the firewall from the Open Web through to the student's academic context. And throw in some ability for educators and academic departments to shape the searching experience, and you then have filters that meet Margaret Hutchins's goal of saving "the time of busy people."

I have focused on the changes in the library most relevant to the higher-education student, but a similar opportunity for the development of advanced filters exists for all library types and their seekers of information. Content providers will need to explicitly build filters that can be tuned and perfected with local knowledge of librarians. Librarians will need to see their role as assembling and tuning the best filters for the learners, citizens, and knowledge workers in their institutions. I see a world in which information providers (publishers, aggregators, and communities of experts) create not just the content but filters as well. In such a world, libraries and librarians will pay increasing attention to sourcing good filters, tuning them to the users in their stewardship. Furthermore, I see librarians expanding their information-literacy programs to include training on understanding filters, how they work, and when or when not to depend on them.

The challenges ahead are well articulated by Anne Blair in her conclusion:

> Whereas early modern reference books were criticized for failing to yield material on a topic of interest, an Internet search invariably offers results. Whether those results are good or not depends on our skills in optimizing searches and assessing results. Those skills themselves will require constant honing, in response to changes in the search engines and in the material available for searching. While a savvy user of early modern reference books needed to be familiar with a fairly stable canon of authors quoted and of finding devices, a skilled Internet user must assess an ever-broadening range of materials that can appear on a list of results, from shopping sites to blogs, from government agencies to elaborate scams. With the digitization of massive amounts of printed matter it will be useful (and perhaps increasingly difficult to younger generations) to understand the tools and categories of the world of print. (Blair 2010, 267–68)

John Dove is president of Credo Reference.

NOTES

1. Joe Janes provided a good citation to this study on the company's website (see: www.keen.com/documents/corpinfo/pressstudy.asp). Unfortunately, the company has taken down that study. The Wayback Machine does allow you to retrieve a summary of the study (http://web.archive.org/web/20010210103715/http://www.keen.com/documents/corpinfo/pressstudy.asp), but I'd love to find a legitimate way to access the full report. This particular unmet need of mine is one I'd gladly pay $50 for.

2. See http://en.wikipedia.org/wiki/American_Chinese_cuisine to learn more about the chop suey sandwich.

3. Video of this speech is available at http://www.youtube.com/watch?v=LabqeJEOQyI .

Chapter Eighteen

Bill Ptacek

In 2020, the public library will be a concept more than a place. The library will be more about what it does for people rather than what it has for people. As society evolves and more content becomes digital, people will access information in different ways. Physical items will be less important than they have been up to now. Library buildings and spaces will be used in different ways, and services will be provided beyond the building and virtually. The library as a catalyst for civic engagement will facilitate learning and growth for people of all ages.

The demand for public libraries has traditionally been driven by the users who walked through the doors. Reference librarians were on hand to answer patron questions primarily using print materials that were carefully collected to be responsive to such inquiries. Young children and their families visited the library to attend story times. Others perused shelves to find information to meet a need or pique an interest. In other words, people came to the *place* to get the *service*.

Over time, access to the library has expanded. Telephone service enabled patrons to find information without having to visit the library. Computer technology ushered in a whole new era that initially tethered patrons to library workstations but gradually cast a wider net so that patrons could use the library virtually by way of the Internet. Titles could be perused online rather than on shelves, and items could be held and picked up at any library location convenient to the patron. Reference services required less involvement by reference librarians as print resources gradually shifted to digital formats, enabling patrons to access information themselves, anytime or anywhere, without having to go through a "gatekeeper" librarian. In general, patrons appreciated the disintermediation of service.

As communication and digital technologies become even more pervasive, libraries will be required to provide content that can be used on whatever is the "device du jour." That means there will be fewer print books on shelves and greater digital content available online. The library lending model of acquiring content for the entire community that can be used and shared by many will work as well with electronic formats as it does for print. Ten years from now, publishers (if they are still in the mix), authors, and content providers, such as Amazon, will recognize libraries as a viable distribution option for digital content that can help them maximize profits and increase the exposure of authors and their work in the same way that bookstores have done over the last century.

As these trends continue to evolve, there will be less programmed space in libraries. As libraries become less about physical access to information, they are more likely to be valued for their importance to the community—as gathering places for civic, educational, and social engagement. The experience of the King County Library System (KCLS) has been that as the size of the collection diminishes, the demand for computer workstations grows. KCLS's libraries have always been full of people, from those studying for the bar exam to others who are homeless and seeking shelter from the elements. Students find libraries convenient places to work on homework or team projects, and community groups rely on the library for meeting spaces.

As new technologies become available, the library will be a place to go, either physically or virtually, to learn. Since the explosion in e-reader sales, KCLS branches are filled with people who want to learn how to use this new technology. The popularity of discussion groups and lecture series creates a great model for lifelong learning, especially for the baby boomer generation that will be well into retirement ten years from now. Similarly, libraries provide tremendous assistance to people who are new to the country. Citizenship classes, English as second language classes, and life-skills programs are all popular in KCLS libraries. As a consequence of offering myriad services to transitional communities, entire families have become loyal library patrons—sometimes spanning several generations.

Libraries can also play a role in virtual learning. There is much work being done on game theory and its uses in education. Libraries are not tied to specific curriculum and can take a leadership role in the development and distribution of software that facilitates learning through the paradigm of games. There is also great promise in the concept of crowd sourcing, a technology that uses computer games to engage large and diverse groups of people to capture information and solutions on a wide variety of issues. Such games have been used to gather input in forums as disparate as genetic research to development of wetlands area.

Public libraries are local, neutral, and respected for providing information that represents different viewpoints. Given its resources and community connections, it is the perfect arena to engage the community in civic discourse on important community issues. With the demise of local news sources, it would be reasonable to assume that local governments, service providers, and community leaders will turn to the library as a venue for discussion and feedback on issues that affect the public. At the same time, this role is consistent with the public's perception of libraries as a trusted source for information and meaningful community participation.

Recently, KCLS offered to initiate a civic-engagement process with the city of Kirkland, a mid-sized community in the KCLS service area. The city, which had acquired a portion of an abandoned railway corridor, wanted to solicit the community's input on the best way to develop the land for public use, which included ideas such as a light-rail line, bike trail, nature trail, or park. The city's usual decision-making process would have been to host a public meeting and gather comments from those attending, which typically are the same few people who attend every public meeting. KCLS's process involved distributing and collecting comment forms at the Kirkland Library, hosting an online public forum, virtual meetings, a design charrette, and a culminating report to the Kirkland City Council. The process garnered input from nearly 700 people, including comments from experts outside the community who were interested in the issue and learned about it through the virtual forum.

Two other crucial areas that will define the public library of the next decade are its role in supporting the information needs of K–12 students and its position to lead community efforts for early-childhood literacy.

Public libraries can help meet the information needs of K–12 students who are affected by the erosion in funding for school libraries. Librarians will work closely with teachers to help them utilize or access information that best fits their curriculum needs. Digital reference materials in public-library collections will be aggregated to fit specific needs or subject areas, and other library educational resources, such as instructional gaming software or the Kahn approach to independent learning, create services and resources perfectly suited to a public library–public school partnership. Outreach vehicles designed as mobile learning labs and stocked with math, science, and technology hardware and software will allow library staff to reach larger numbers of students at school and after-school sites. As schools face increasing pressure to achieve better student test scores, the library can provide materials and tutoring on test-taking techniques and other academic competencies required of youngsters who are entering the world of standardized tests. The KCLS Study Zone program is a free tutoring service offered after school and on weekends where students can work with a Study Zone tutor on a drop-in basis or by scheduled visit. Some sites also offer smart tables that utilize subject-based software geared toward group study sessions.

This popular program is entirely supported by a broad network of KCLS volunteers.

Early-childhood development and early literacy are recognized as major elements in the success of students, schools, and, ultimately, the community. It is now proven that a child's ability to read and learn is primarily formed by age five. Organizations such as United Way and other nonprofits have made early literacy the focus of many community-wide efforts to ensure that all children start school ready to learn. In today's world, most preschool learning happens in daycares, including home-based daycares, and public libraries are well positioned to use mobile outreach vehicles to reach home daycare providers, parents, and caregivers to provide reading-readiness programs for children under the age of five. In ten years, schools will recognize how crucial this issue is to their success and will work closely with children's librarians, who have great expertise in early-childhood development, to identify areas in the community where the public library can make a difference.

The next decade's librarian will spend less time dealing with the physical aspects of content, for example, labeling, shelving, or checking out items, and more time acting as consultant to the general public. Librarian as information expert will become librarian as psychologist or sociologist. Instead of being the gatekeepers to limited sources of information, they will have to be able to comb through vast amounts of data to find just the right information for the patron. Understanding the patron and linking that understanding to relevant content will be the art of librarianship. And all of this will take place inside the library, outside the library, or virtually.

It is imperative that the public library remain relevant to the people it serves. In the future, libraries will be less about services and more about how to be of service. Research on patron interests and behavior patterns will be crucial to this effort, and libraries will have to be adept at marketing and customer-insight techniques. If libraries can continue to stay ahead of the curve on new technologies and improve the patron experience, they will ensure the value of the library for the next generation.

Bill Ptacek is the director of the King County Library System, which was the busiest library in the United States in 2010 and named Library Journal's *2011 Library of the Year.*

Chapter Nineteen

Loriene Roy

The library in 2020 will be the setting I hope to find and the place that I cannot yet imagine. It will be a customizable space—physical and virtual—that replicates and extends the glamour, intrigue, and comfort of the many libraries I have visited over the years. Thus, it is a place of potential as well as a place of confirmed assuredness: it will offer the range of services that are seen in today's libraries and serve as a laboratory where patrons can be themselves and not only encounter existing information but also create, share, and learn together.

Dr. Gregory Cajete has written extensively on building educational models based on indigenous worldviews. My library of the future will enable patrons to find fulfillment along the lines of Cajete's orientation cycle, as described in his book *Look to the Mountain: An Ecology of Indigenous Education* (Cajete 1997, 23). This involves a cycle of actions, starting with being and extending to asking, seeking, making, having, sharing, and celebrating. All of these actions can be completed by the individual but can also be enhanced when adopted by a group or a community. My library of the future will help me lead a fulfilled life.

BEING: A PLACE FOR UNDERSTANDING SELF

My library of the future is a place where one can find security and acclamation. It will also be a challenging place that affords discovery and transformation of oneself. It will support one's worldview.

Support of the mind will also be balanced through support of the body and wellness. My library will be a place where patrons and library staff can strengthen and renew their health. This will be seen in the aura of the site that offers the refreshing surroundings of new knowledge and the social space to entertain and meet outside of oneself. The building itself will be situated on the land in a way that supports one's physicality and spirit.

The library of the future will support its library workers, affirming the motto of the ALA Allied Professional Association: "Libraries work because we do." There will be attention paid to workplace wellness. Like the library of Tallinn (Estonia) University of Technology, there will be a sauna for staff use along with a massage chair. In addition, staff will have access to a recumbent bicycle, a small lap pool, and a changing room with shower. The public areas of the library will include an exercise space where yoga mats can be spread out, a large screen on which staff can project exercise videos, and a stage from which a trainer could lead group aerobics or dance classes. Wellness materials would include spa facilities where one can make appointments with a rotating group of masseurs with options for manicures and/or pedicures. The library will support social-media connections with area specialists; each day staff members could receive a tweet from Dr. Barbara Bergin, orthopedic surgeon, reminding you of the simple actions you can take to prevent maladies such as plantar fasciitis.

ASKING: A PLACE TO QUESTION YOURSELF AND OTHERS

The library space will support the continual redesign of its interior, reflecting the spectrum of patron needs. Before noon, the design will be especially accommodating to the homeless, young parents, homeschoolers, and the retired. It will adjust its interior to welcome after-schoolers, the business crowd, and college students, as well as to their individual changing needs ranging from browsing to independent study and group experience.

The library will provide social space for meet-up groups, formal and informal classes, and a trusted, safe place for online dating partners to communicate and meet. It will provide travel assistance and recommendations similar to WAYN (Where Are You Now), which allows library patrons to leave suggestions for local and other travel planning. Like the Auckland (Aotearoa/New Zealand) Public Library, information on the world will be offered in an open news area that features a large-screen television airing news from international sources, access to international newspapers, and language-study options, including space for language café gatherings for small meet-up groups. It will be possible for language classes to be downloaded onto personal devices as well.

My library will be my one-stop location outside of home and work. Here is where I will conduct the bank services that I cannot do online, renew my driver's license, get or renew a passport, mail or ship, connect with city services, and find referrals for local services.

SEEKING: A PLACE TO WAYFIND THROUGH ITS
ARCHITECTURE AND DESIGN

From entrance to exit, the library space will offer both the sense of homeland and of exciting and far-flung travel. The footprint of the library will be placed in accordance with the four directions. Creative knowledge will flow in from the cardinal directions—the east will bring the new learning of art and poetry, the north will bring the strength of leadership, the west will bring spirituality, and the south will bring teachings and philosophies. The library would feature green spaces and be LEED-construction qualified. The HVAC system would be built, like that of the Bozeman (Montana) Public Library, to naturally cool or warm the interior. Like the Hennepin County (Minnesota) Library, the library roof will be a green space where grasses and trees grow.

The pattern in the carpet at the main Auckland Public Library replicates the maps that the indigenous peoples of the land, the Maori, used in their ocean navigations that brought them to Aotearoa/New Zealand, the land of the long white cloud. The floor coverings of my library in 2020 would connect the physical space to the land, allowing human visitors to place themselves in the continuum of history.

The building will feature the words and songs of the people. Lights on the elevator in the Hennepin County Library spell out words—search terms that people are using while navigating the online catalog and/or words appearing in titles of books being circulated. The library of the future will glow with the energies of many minds coming together. The lighting system will represent the seeking minds and also the universe. Like the Saami parliamentary library in Karasjok, Norway, the lighting will replicate the array of stars in the Milky Way and be a navigational beacon during winter evenings. The walls of that library are inscribed with the text of cultural adages, a wall of wooden lathwork. And the walls and glass will display text from indigenous languages. Like the Bozeman Public Library, there will be windows facing a woodland and river and a bird-watcher's station complete with binoculars, birding books, and a sketch book.

The library will offer spaces to linger and read. It will host a lathed reading garden in a garden moat, like that found at the Parklands (TeKete-Wananga o WaiMokihi) Library, a branch of the Christchurch (New Zealand) Public Library. The green roof will also provide a rooftop reading room like that found at the JüriRaamatukogu (combined school and public library) in Harju County, Estonia. The teen space will be as spacious as the McAllen (Texas) Public Library's building, a renovated Walmart. There will, of course, be Wi-Fi, outlets, and charging stations both inside and outside the building that match the current technology and trends.

There will be quiet space, providing an option for study, reading, or contemplation. Like the Queensland State Library in Brisbane, Australia, and the Cultural Resources Center of the National Museum of the American Indian, the library will have a ceremonial space. The outdoor space will be the venue for a variety of self-reflective practices including cowboy church services, jazz mass, the blessing of animals, and a labyrinth.

And there will be a cafeteria—like the National Museum of American Indian's Mitsitam Café. The menu will feature local and traditional foods, much of which would be grown onsite in raised gardening beds. I will be able to buy and eat wild-rice salad whenever I want.

MAKING: THE PLACE WHERE WE COME TO CREATE

My library will host a laboratory with a teaching space. This is a place to learn technology skills one-on-one. There will be multimedia work stations such as those in the Fine Arts Library at the University of Texas at Austin where I can find the equipment and training to do such tasks as convert audio tapes to digital formats. There will be a recording studio because my library will be located in Austin, Texas, the live music capital of the world. Of course, there will be several live-music stages that host performances and karaoke in and outside of the facility. There will be listening stations. People can record their lives or interview others at the oral-history station. This is where people can add personal commentary about community history or create their own oral-history initiatives. All interviews will be automatically and instantly transcribed and indexed. I will be able to join a group to study and converse in other languages. The library will have a printing station like the Bibliotheca Alexandrina in Egypt where books are printed—and bound—to order. Outside of the library will be a community garden space where I can learn to grown and maintain my own food sources. Cooking classes can take place within and outside the building.

HAVING: WHAT WE OWN AND SAMPLE

My library offers information in a wide range of formats from text to audio to video to digital. The staff selects a collection that promotes serendipity while responding to my own reading tastes by supplying customized services. Readers have options to support and advise each other through message boards, social meetings, meet-ups, and reading advice. It is a place to welcome authors into the circle of being as we participate in their creative process when they share their content, their motivations, and personal aspects of their lives. There will be a writing lounge—a space for writers to gather resources and for aspiring writers to meet with visiting agents. Writing opportunities—including grants—will be advertised and proofing or editing services provided. Unique materials will be housed in special collections.

There will be a life-arts area, much like the one in the Dongguan Public Library in China, where I can find cookbooks and decorating resources as well as advice to maintain one's personal living space. Here will be a tool-lending collection where I can check out a push lawn mower, a large ladder, a rotor tiller, or a shovel and receive instructions on their use. There will be robots—like the ones at the University of Kentucky that retrieve books stored in bins so that nearby storage offers access to material not available for browsing. The robots will provide endless entertainment and reduce over-use strains on the part of library workers.

SHARING: A SPACE TO SHOWCASE OURSELVES

The exhibit space will feature physical and online exhibits curated by the library staff or created for sharing by the public. There will be a performance space for puppetry and plays like that of the Nashville Public Library. Group facilities will be available for television viewing, especially for sports events. The library café will be open during these events, and alcohol will be served.

CELEBRATING: THE PLACE TO COME TOGETHER AND COMMEMORATE OUR LIVES AND ACHIEVEMENTS

Finally, my library will truly be the third living space, the place between home and work that entices the daily stop for refreshment and encouragement. Ample, safe parking is available, and my tire pressure and car fluids levels will be checked upon request. It is the place that we will mark on our calendars, for it is here where my favorite live music will ring, where people will gather to celebrate themselves and others, and where the future is assured. Library patrons will be celebrated when their accomplishments are mentioned in local news outlets, when their birthdays are noted, and when they announce good news through social media. And if I cannot physically visit the library, I can participate through Web conferencing and will receive frequent updates via social networks. The library of the future is our new hometown where we are known, remembered, forgiven, and welcomed.

Loriene Roy is a professor at the School of Information, University of Texas at Austin.

BIBLIOGRAPHY

Cajete, Gregory. *Look to the Mountain: An Ecology of Indigenous Education*. Skyland, NC: Kivaki, 1997.

V

Leadership and Vision

Chapter Twenty

Josie Barnes Parker

The library in 2020 will offer a culture of generosity supported by fiscal oversight that reflects rigorous controls and realistic projections.

The key to operating generously with a conservative budget process lies with leadership. When institutions, businesses, and nonprofits operate within their scope, and within their budgets, they earn the respect and trust of their communities. Over the long haul, that trust and respect translates into funding support. This is true no matter how an institution is structured and governed. There is plenty of noise right now in the library industry about threats and challenges, but there is always noise. The library in 2020 will succeed in its community when it operates well above the noise, where people can hear one another speak and where communication occurs.

I came into my current position just over ten years ago on the heels of a financial scandal that rocked our community and our library system. The financial mess, while complicated, was straightforward enough in terms of the process for getting things in order. However, the broken faith and lack of trust in the community has taken years to recover. The decision to give back as much as possible to the community through library services and facilities, while restructuring the financial operations of the system, led to what we call a culture of generosity that invests all of our decisions, from the mundane to the strategic.

Because we had to question all of our practices and assumptions, we confronted our bias about what libraries are supposed to do or not do. In many cases, that bias did not reflect how the library was being used nor what our community told us they wanted in their library. Questioning and challenging that bias was key to this system positioning itself to serve its community well into the twenty-first century. In many ways, the ripples of decisions made a decade ago are still felt as we consider how to move through the second decade of this century, prepared to be relevant in the third decade. I likely won't be involved in 2020, but I would offer the following as guides for leaders in 2020.

The first is about what I call budget view. When I hear or read about library budgets that are essentially fixed because library service is fixed and determined by history, contracts, or accepted practice, I cringe. That library is in trouble—not because it has less revenue but because leaders are looking backward at the budget. I realize that libraries structured within larger governmental units have constraints that individual taxing units such as the system I am in now do not have. However, the leader of a successful library in 2020, no matter the structure, will tear that budget to pieces and put it back together and restructure the library accordingly, if need be, to make good work happen within that budget. View the budget through the lens of the future. What does this budget need to allow the library to deliver good service over the next five years? Ten years? What changes have to occur, and when, to accomplish service that is relevant to its community? If we focus on what we need to do in the future while we are looking at our current finances, we can make the case for funding changes ahead of the need.

The second is to understand how power is manifested in your community. Withholding service from a paying public may work in the short term, but communities have long memories. Using leverage that we really don't have to try to make a case for relevance is an expensive gambit that, in my opinion, is simply not worth the cost. I spent a summer driving my mother-in-law around a rural county in Mississippi over thirty years ago so that she could lobby county supervisors for funding for a public library. I became exasperated and angry with some of the comments made to her by people she had known all of her adult life, and I was angry with her for not giving them a piece of her mind. Her counsel to me that summer has stood me in very good stead: never mistake who in the conversation holds the power. If you are asking for something, it is not you. Libraries generally are asking, and our leaders need to understand power and how it is wielded in a community in order to ask the right people at the right time and, especially, to know when we cannot, and should not, ask. If we are focusing on the long term, being strategic when applying for more support is a sign of a healthy institution led thoughtfully and carefully.

Last, and perhaps the most important, is to simply be generous. The library's money is not the library's money; it is a pooled resource funded by many people who for many different reasons value library service in the community and by some who do not value library service. While it is not feasible or sustainable to be all things to all people, it is feasible and sustainable to offer something for everyone. Generosity is cheap. It is a state of mind that when freely offered through services, policies, and facility design is recognized as respect for the paying community. How that respect is returned in support is dependent on many factors, but it is returned. If it is the long haul that we are focusing on, and if we are viewing our budget through the lens of the future, we will adjust accordingly and do good work within our budget with sincere generosity.

The funding crisis across the country affects everyone and everything. Libraries are one of many, but we are usually the only one of our kind in a community. The year 2020 will see libraries financially recovering all across the country. The opportunity to offer respect through generosity and rigorous financial control will be one that library leaders will leverage without hesitation.

Josie Barnes Parker is director of the Ann Arbor District Library.

Chapter Twenty-One

Mary Ann Mavrinac

The library in 2020 will be a tale of two academic research libraries: one flourishing in the best of times and one languishing in the worst of times. In the words of Charles Dickens:

> It was the best of times, it was the worst of times, it was the age of wisdom, it was the age of foolishness, it was the epoch of belief, it was the epoch of incredulity, it was the season of Light, it was the season of Darkness, it was the spring of hope, it was the winter of despair, we had everything before us, we had nothing before us. (Dickens 1859, 3)

In this work of fiction[1], in 2012, our two research libraries are both situated in tier-one research institutions established over 175 years ago, steeped in tradition yet vying for the attention of students who are increasingly opting for an online, global education over a residential university experience. Both libraries are housed in iconic spaces traditionally defined by the depth and scale of their collections. Deep traditions and symbolic rituals inherent in iconic research libraries add weight to the challenges of *transforming* these libraries to meet the needs of twenty-first-century researchers and learners. Adding to this challenge are the complexities and elusiveness of achieving transformational change encapsulated by James MacGregor Burns:

> to cause a metamorphosis in form or structure, a change in the very condition or nature of a thing, a change into another substance, a radical change in outward form or inner character. (Burns 2003, 24)

The library in pursuit of the best of times looked ahead to 2020 and then looked back to 2005. Seven years ahead. Seven years back. How had teaching changed over the past seven years? How had research changed? How had technology, content, publishing, and social platforms changed over the past seven years? How had academic research libraries changed over the past seven years? Were they keeping pace within the broader environment? Within the university? The library in the best of times believed it had fallen behind. It decided to pursue a new future by 2020. It believed there was no other option or it risked falling even more behind. Over several years, it methodically went about the complex task of achieving transformational change.

In contrast, the library in the worst of times was convinced that the changes it had made were enough. It was convinced that the centrality of the research library would endure.

Herein lies a tale of two libraries . . .

THE LIBRARY IN THE BEST OF TIMES

The library in the best of times in 2020 is a physical and virtual collaborative hub sustained by an immensely talented staff driving innovation and in perpetual learning mode (Schein 2004). The library's culture is steeped in collaboration from its core principles to its daily actions. The tagline for the library is "The Power of C"—collaboration! The library's very being is imbued with a collaborative state of mind.

What does this mean for the library? Starting from its foundational principles, the work of the library is collaborative, team based, and project focused. The library in the best of times realized years ago that a sustainable, enriching future required a complete retooling of its entire operations. It had to look at its values, culture, structure, operations, processes, reward systems, and vision, realizing that life as a traditional academic research library was no longer viable, much less interesting. There was no perceived major external threat that precipitated this change for the library in the best of times. There was no magic bullet that would ensure an enriching future. There was no pot of money to dip into to pave the way or to ease the pain. It was a combination of great leadership, intense foundational work, trust, teamwork, risk-taking, innovation, and learning, all of which were critical to the achievement of an enriching and sustainable future in the academy.

Why did the library in the best of times have the courage to aspire to a new future state? In a word, it was trust. The library's organization had evolved to a model of shared leadership. The organization embraced the higher order values of integrity, openness, diversity, equality, fairness, and the pursuit of happiness (Burns 2003). Values-based leadership and values-based decision making engendered trust among organizational members. Moreover, the organization placed learning and its inherent mistakes and failures as a central organizational asset and established capacity building as a strategic priority. It took to heart the words of Edgar Schein when he said:

> We basically do not know what the world of tomorrow will be like, except that it will be *different*, more *complex*, more *fast*-paced, and more *culturally diverse*. This means that organizations *and their leaders will have to become perpetual learners*. (Schein 2004, 393)

During the years leading up to 2020, all library staff were expected to contribute to this new collaborative reality. In so doing, all were provided opportunities to learn new skills, take risks, and drive innovative collaborative initiatives.

But before this could happen, the library had to turn inward to align basic organizational processes with this new reality of collaboration. How could the library be a collaborative engine for its community when it did not collaborate internally, when departmental cultures continued to define the organizational psyche, and when traditional roles comprised the organization's fabric? How would new needs be met, new roles be filled, and new projects be driven if organizational processes continued along traditional, functional lines?

The library embarked upon a complete review of its basic operations. It decided which operations must be retained and performed locally, which must be shared with collaborative partners regionally, nationally, or internationally, which must cease, and which could be performed by another business unit on campus or otherwise. This was difficult, time-consuming, and emotionally draining work, but the goal was lofty: free up and reallocate resources to embrace new roles for a sustainable future. This painstaking work occurred over several years.

Some staff faced with the elimination of their work function felt the pain of their identity and value erased by a future that was unknown. But the library placed a high value on the health and well-being of its employees, investing heavily in a variety of support systems to assist with the emotional elements of transitioning to a new role. Moreover, it invested in learning and development as it placed learning as a central organizational asset. Capacity building meant that the hearts and minds of all organizational members were included in developing the library that would flourish in the best of times. Notwithstanding, a few people opted to leave or to retire as the nature of work was changing in ways that that were not in accordance with their interests and talent.

There were many times when going back to "the way we were" tugged at the library's resolve. It was easy to see why most academic research libraries in 2020 looked very similar to those in 2000 or 1990 (or 1980). The furniture may have been rearranged, but nothing had fundamentally changed. These were the libraries languishing in the worst of times as they chose the easy route of minimal change.

The library in the best of times faced numerous other tasks and challenges: what would faculty think when collections were no longer acquired and inventoried in a traditional manner or kept onsite "just in case"? How would the library reach the best of times when faculty might collectively forestall collaborative solutions to collection building, solutions that would mean offsite regional print repositories, primarily digital collections, and a very small onsite print collection that was mainly unique, rare, and special? How would the library defend itself when the very nature of a research library would be called into question if it no longer was defined by its collections?

In the spirit of openness, the library demonstrated exemplary leadership in working with its faculty to identify a variety of options to meet their many and varied research needs while at the same time making the case for a new, more enriching, and sustainable future. Using evidence, it established its core mission of underpinning the teaching, learning, and research mission of the academy. It developed an advocacy strategy that equipped all library staff with the means and the messages that were in alignment with the library's collaborative future. And it proved itself indispensable by illustrating the integral value of expert tools, products, content, and spaces, as well as expediting and enriching the research, teaching, and learning of faculty and students. Library staff had expertise that was in demand, and it had a modus that was valued: collaboration. Resources were readily shared with the library because it was willingly sharing its resources, adding value to the academy.

The library as place continued to dominate as the symbolic center of knowledge at the campus. Increasingly, as virtual reality blurred "actual" reality, the library was an important touchstone of "knowledge" in an otherwise fluid environment. Through its doors, the library—physically and virtually—was an agora, a gathering space for collaborative activities, experiential learning, research activity, and, when needed, solitude. Research hubs and stations peppered open spaces; niche and intimate spaces were tucked away in relation to programmatic focus. Immersive environments, multisurface computing, and intelligent design and content provided experiential opportunities for creative expression, sense making, and knowledge creation. Spaces for sanctuary and reflection were sought amid an increasingly chaotic world where private "public" space was a rarity. The combination of spaces, technology, expertise, and content was a potent elixir when integrated into the teaching, learning, and research activities of the academy. The academic research library was flourishing in the best of times.

Many staff work areas were in the open where faculty and students could see and engage with them. These impromptu exchanges were stimulating, rewarding, and often led to opportunities for the library. Other staff worked within research hubs or as part of teams in different areas of the university, yet others were part of virtual collaborative hubs comprised of international research teams or in support of global learning in an online environment.

Special collections moved to an area of prominence, no longer behind closed doors. Unique books and manuscripts were of immense interest, a catalyst for research, integration into the curriculum, student internships, and user-driven content. The semantic Web enabled relational connection of born digital and digitized collections throughout the world spawning a renaissance in humanistic research, paralleling the massive collaborative research effort in the sciences. The library supported this with a vibrant digital scholarship and publishing program. But unlike the sciences, the content was provided by, primarily, libraries, museums, and archives. The library's focus on collaborative collecting and acquiring digital collections provided the means to obtain more specialized, unique, and rare collections that supplied the content and data for research and teaching and to curate and steward born digital materials. No longer was faculty concerned about the library's perceived inattention to collection building. The library was increasingly viewed as an indispensable partner in the academy. As a partner, the library automatically became a collaborator for research opportunities, grant funding, and technology-transfer initiatives. The result: the library had other sources of funding beyond its operating budget. The library in the best of times used its discretionary funds to drive innovation, transform its virtual and physical spaces, and invest in its staff. The library was vibrant, energized, and a magnet for opportunity. Such is the power of collaboration!

THE LIBRARY IN THE WORST OF TIMES

Witness the library in the worst of times. This library stayed the course. In so doing, it continued to fall behind. In not making a choice to change how it fundamentally operated, it made a choice, one that resulted in a slow but steady decline. At times, the decline was imperceptible, leading staff to believe that all was well. Others increasingly viewed the library as retrograde, seeing it as an easy mark to offset university budgetary pressures. As such, resources became scarce as operating budgets were incrementally reduced. Instead of changing course, the library in the worst of times continued doing much of the same activities. It occasionally made superficial changes or piloted programs that provided a jolt of creative energy, but nothing marked or fundamental changed. Over the years, there were several one-off collaborations, but these were mainly initiated by a few library staff who understood the importance of collaboration in support of the academic mission. Scarce resources spawned suspicion between library departments as each closed ranks to hoard what resources each had. Rumor was rampant. Which area would be cut next? Will it be me who loses my job? Jealousy, envy, gossip, and assumptions undermined the health of the library as morale plummeted.

Staff continued to build collections "just in case" from their offices. Traditional services such as reference and circulation were cosmetically changed, such as the provision of research consultations and chat reference a few hours per day. Librarians continued to believe that they were the experts in research and reference. While musing: "If only students would ask," these librarians ignored the technologies and applications used matter-of-factly by students throughout their grade-school and secondary-school years.

This is not to say that the library wasn't busy. The physical library in the worst of times in 2020 was extremely crowded and hectic as students choosing a residential university experience needed a place to study and hang out. Campus administrators viewed this activity with increasing skepticism, seeing the academic library as a glorified study hall and an expensive one at that! Metrics indicated that circulation of materials continued to decline, yet the library continued to ask for more space for its collections. On campus, space was a finite resource. Other campus units demanded more square footage for undergraduate research opportunities, experiential learning, and collaborative group activities. Many eyed the library as a logical future home. Library staff were unnerved by this, arguing that students needed a place to study and that collections, as central to the research needs of faculty, needed space to grow. Suspicion abounded.

The library's virtual spaces were perfunctory, offering a passive Web presence that provided informational items such as hours of service, lists of subject librarians, lists of subject guides, and descriptions of services. Library staff dabbled in social media but did not weave it into the fabric of their communications, as they believed it was not scholarly or professional.

In 2020, the library in the worst of times realized it was too late when campus administration gave notice that the library would close with essential services outsourced, that the physical space would be used for other academic purposes, and that digital resources would be obtained by other means. Like a dying patient who realizes, too late, that the life they led contributed to their imminent passing, library staff realized they had played it safe—so safe that it put the research library at risk. In spite of several warnings, it failed to transform itself. And now it would close, ending a 182-year history.

A tale of two libraries: *It was a season of Light, it was the season of Darkness.*

Mary Ann Mavrinac is vice provost and Andrew H. and Janet Dayton Neilly Dean, River Campus Libraries, University of Rochester.

BIBLIOGRAPHY

Burns, James MacGregor. *Transforming Leadership: A New Pursuit of Happiness*. New York: Atlantic Monthly Press, 2003.
Dickens, Charles. *A Tale of Two Cities*. 1859. Reprint, New York: Dodd, Mead, 1942.
Schein, Edgar. H. *Organizational Culture and Leadership*. 3rd ed. San Francisco: Jossey-Bass 2004.

NOTE

1. This is a work of fiction, a hypothetical look at two "generic" research libraries.

Chapter Twenty-Two

Peter Morville

The library in 2020 is the last bastion of truth. Sure, you can search yottaby-tes of free data by simply batting an eyelash. But it's dangerous to believe what you see through the iGlass lens. As you learned the hard way back in the Facebook era, if you're not paying for it, you are the product. That research study about the safety and efficacy of Lipitor Lollipops was sponsored by a subsidiary of a subsidiary of Pfizer. That consultant you almost hired wrote his own customer reviews. And while you can't tell for sure because the algorithms are opaque, it sure seems like the first page of Web search is pay-to-play. You routinely skip past the top ten results.

Unfortunately, this state of corruption isn't limited to the Web. Politicians are in the pocket of lobbyists. Doctors push pills for profit. Teachers and bank clerks work on commission. And journalists? Well, they don't really exist. And neither does evolution, climate change, or Newton's law of gravity.

Polarization was solved by personalization. Now, people learn their own truths. We should have known back in 2015, when the ratio of adults who believe "God created humans in their present form within the last 10,000 years" hit 51 percent, that we had passed a tipping point. At least we're not burning witches at the stake, except in Texas, which doesn't really count.

The good news is we still have the library. In a world that won't stop spinning, it's the one place you can go for truth. Their articles, books, and databases are mostly ad free. And librarians are the folks you can trust. Is it safe to ride your bicycle to work? Do vegans live longer? Which refrigerator has the best privacy controls? And why does your self-driving car sometimes take the long route home? Librarians help you find the best answers. As a result, you make informed decisions, and over time, all this learning adds up to improve not only your quality of life but also your longevity.

The bad news is nobody uses the library anymore. Most folks are too busy or too lazy to venture beyond the fast food of the free Web. Plus, they have absolutely no idea what they're missing. While many schools and colleges make half-hearted attempts to integrate information literacy into their curricula, only the best students learn much from these tutorials. If their brains fail to explode when the librarian begins speaking in Boolean, their patience surely runs out when told they must know, before they start to search, which database (*of dozens, each with unique interfaces and query languages*) contains the answer to their question.

It didn't have to be this way. There was a time, not so long ago, when librarians had the chance to change the future. People's infatuation with Google had begun to ebb. They were hungry for something better. If libraries had offered a good alternative—an integrated search and discovery tool that enabled fast, easy access to popular content, scientific research, and scholarly sources—we might have moved forward, not back. We almost did.

Those "Web-scale discovery tools" with single search boxes, faceted navigation interfaces, and aggregated indexes brought us so close to success. But many of the older, more powerful faculty and librarians resisted this "dumbing down." They preferred the native database interfaces because only they knew how to use them. And, thanks to the squabbling of database vendors and the greed of journal publishers, seamless access to full-text content remained a mirage. There were a few brilliant open-discovery projects at the crossroads of open source and open access, but librarians lacked the money, power, and resolve to scale and sustain these systems.

To be fair, librarians got a lot of things right. After a period of panic about the shift from physical to digital, folks realized the power of "library as place" is timeless and unbound by technology or format. Universities and cities built a new generation of libraries to serve not only as cathedrals of knowledge but also as comfortable, collaborative spaces for learning and co-creation. Most included room for books, which is lucky considering that e-books remain subject to format wars, legal ambiguities, viral contagion, and high prices.

At the same time, the lens of "library as people" launched an army of embedded librarians into departments, classrooms, and online courses. Their integration into student and faculty workflow dramatically improved the real and perceived value of librarians. And each time they helped a patron find and evaluate information, they improved that person's learning skills for life.

There was even a big move toward the vision of "library as platform." Noble geeks developed elaborate schemata for open-source, open-API, open-access environments with linked data and semantic markup to unleash innovation and integration through transparency, crowd-sourcing, and mash-ups. They waxed poetic about the potential of Web analytics and cloud computing to uncover implicit relationships and emerging patterns, identify scholarly pathways and lines of inquiry, and connect and contextualize artifacts with adaptive algorithms. They promised ecosystems of participation and infrastructures for the creation and sharing of knowledge and culture.

Unfortunately, the folks controlling the purse strings had absolutely no idea what these geeks were talking about, and they certainly weren't about to entrust the future of their libraries (and their own careers) to the same bunch of incompetent techies who had systematically failed, for more than ten years, to simply make the library's search box work like Google.

So, that's how we landed in 2020 in Pottersville rather than Bedford Falls. It's not that the truth doesn't exist. It's just hard to find. If you live in a wealthy town or work for a major university, you're likely to have a good library. And, if you know where to look and how to search, you're able to make informed decisions that improve your life. But most folks lack access and know-how, so they stick to tradition, trust their gut, fail to learn, and fall behind.

It wasn't supposed to end this way. The story of the library was rags to riches, not the rich get richer. Andrew Carnegie nailed it back in 1889. His commitment toward the establishment of free libraries derived from the firm belief that "a library outranks any other one thing a community can do to benefit its people. It is a never failing spring in the desert."

Now, for many, that spring has failed. We've left our kids with Grickle Grass instead of Truffula Trees. What's most disturbing is that we had all the puzzle pieces: beautiful physical spaces, vast digital collections, powerful algorithms, and usable interfaces. We talked about service design and cross-channel user experience. But we never walked the walk.

Some said it was all about information, while others obsessed about architecture. The part we missed was the whole.

A library is an act of inspiration architecture. It lifts us up, not only by enabling our search for the truth but also by serving as a symbol of past accomplishment and future potential. It reminds us that the path to discovery isn't always, or even usually, a straight line. It invites us, in the interplay between physical and digital, to explore strange connections between intellect and emotion, wisdom and knowledge, mind and body.

A library, like a national park, teaches us that we all benefit when our most valuable treasures are held in common. In the wonderful and wacky intertwingularity of information and architecture, it inspires us to better ourselves. If only we'd put it all together, back then, when we had the chance.

Peter Morville is president, Semantic Studios.

Chapter Twenty-Three

Daniel Chudnov

The library in 2020 will be crumbling.

The library today is failing; in the next few years, it will fail. Having failed, those of us who know well what the library once was will, upon revisiting it years later, be confronted with repurposed ruins, the odd shape of which makes sense only in a forgotten retrospect. We may tell stories, we may mount informative plaques, but the cracks and fissures of architectural features that once defined the library will be ignored and allowed to deepen and combine, "Free to fall."

I do not relish this thought, but I have no other.

We are failing on several fronts: collections, services, and imagination. Each of these failures makes our libraries resemble frail or crippled members of feral animal packs, ripe for the kill in the eyes of predators. In 2017 or 2018, a business program on whatever remains of public television will recount how one industry after another separated our core functions from each other, attacked each in consumer, corporate, and political marketplaces, and left our remains for scavengers to fight over like so many nature shows.

I do not look forward to this, but I cannot look backward, either.

It hurts too much to look backward. In my brief fifteen-year career, our largest and proudest institutions encouraged and promulgated licensing schemes that willingly gutted our most basic principles of resource sharing. We've cancelled paper subscriptions en masse and turned over our budgets to a handful of conglomerating remote providers whose profit margins we inflate in exchange for the one-way trap of e-resources, telling ourselves that by securing "dark archive" copies we've purchased sufficient insurance. We sit idle while device manufacturers convince our communities that it is easier to purchase rights-restricted copies of media for instant use than it is to delay gratification, purchase, borrow, and lend copies freely, and the only major initiatives to convert textbook purchasing over to bulk e-book purchases barely save students enough to be worthwhile.

It is easy to watch the numbers turn away from us. Each fall, the students arriving on our college campuses carry newer, sleeker devices with better screens, batteries, and user experiences for knowledge acquisition than anything we offer. As our own collection resources prove difficult to use on these devices, the lure of commodity purchasing of restricted-use copies without our assistance or intervention turns from a threat to a best practice. Maybe it already has turned. The largest device makers enable thousands of apps to bloom, but they take a cut of each sale, and they define the terms allowed for each content purchase, and we have no leverage in what has never even approximated a discussion about how our libraries might fit this equation. Sure, we fought off SOPA (Stop Online Piracy Act), but the U.S. public domain is still stuck at 1922, and each new purchase with a major vendor locks each individual purchaser deeper into that vendor's closed ecosystem. There is no cultural willpower to fight this. There is no pending class-action lawsuit demanding that device and app and content vendors allow competitors' content to work on their devices or demanding that consumers be empowered to take their content with them off one platform and onto another or demanding legalization of resale marketplaces where individuals and small businesses can trade purchased media freely.

At the same time, we ship our physical holdings to off-site facilities shared across institutions, weeding out multiple copies along the way, thinning their ranks and making them less available than before, all the while turning our buildings into charging stations with good Wi-Fi and coffee access. There is no end game here that reflects well on librarians or offers a reason to visit our collections.

Except for special collections. But even here, we face a bleak future. As justification thins for retaining desirable physical spaces devoted to a bygone ideal of "library," the heaviest remaining anchors are "what makes us unique." Unique though our special collections may be, they also fall prey to the space crunches and off-site shelving transitions and limited access patterns relative to what's Googleable. The economic pattern seems obvious. The turnover from stacks to user spaces pushes more and more collections—special and otherwise—to shared facilities. The removal of library-like materials and functions from our hollowed-out buildings supports a steady trickle of formal shutdowns of local library budgets, with functions turned over to the entities operating the shared facilities. The shared facilities, if sufficiently shrewd, might grow in stature, offering new economies of scale as the previous "member" institutions stumble. The shared facilities themselves start to merge and conglomerate, turning into or over to more profit-oriented ventures that sell their wares back to our institutions at ever-higher prices, to be purchased by savings gained from local library operations lost.

If you argue that Google's book scanning efforts already did this, another might counter that a previous generation of microfilming efforts had already beat Google to the punch, with the only salient differences being scale and responsiveness. Turning this backward-focused line of argument around toward the near future, picture our consortia eating our distinct collections and, not yet sated, gorging on each other, and you'll see we've long since set ourselves down this path. The lucky institutions among ours will end up franchises of a handful of pseudo-competitive, oligopoly market makers. If, that is to say, we aren't already.

Then there are the services we provide online: from search, which everyone likes to do across everything except us, where we limit searches to what we have locally, to delivery, where so many of us still put arcane forms and data-entry tasks between our users and what they want from us. Why wouldn't you skip all that and just buy something yourself, especially if you can search at a bigger scale and acquire what you wish for only a few dollars, delivered right to you? And our "resolver" screens are an obstacle course of circa-1999 user-experience minimalism, backed by knowledge bases of varied accuracy and quality. We have an appalling lack of user-experience integration among the subscribed resources and Web-based services we provide. Countless jobs are posted daily to library lists calling for more people with new generations of technical skills to addresses these issues, but our schools aren't turning out code-, design-, and user-experience-skilled librarians to fill them. Junior systems staff aren't getting the mentoring and peer support they need to develop and mature, and experienced staff in traditional functions seeking to level up their technical chops are left foundering without meaningful support structures. Senior leadership at many of our organizations rose up before these skills were even defined. And despite famously right-skewed demographics, we've done little to prepare a new generation of leadership to point in these new directions. We cannot afford to hire the best leaders from the tech world. Our role as librarians, serving our communities at the intersection of the information needs and changing technologies, is no less important, but we are ill equipped to keep up with changes in needs and changes in technologies, and more than ever our users adopt new solutions before we even learn of them. With vanishing collections and insufficient tooling and staff to bridge the gap between collections and services we offer and our community members relative to what they can acquire efficiently for themselves already, support for more traditional education and research services we traditionally bundled alongside and enabled through our collections and services will erode as well.

Our chaotic messes in collections and services do not drive us toward failure as quickly as our lack of imagination. We do not reconsider how to organize ourselves, maintaining traditional distinctions between departments and functions despite many of us having more crosscutting projects than before. Many of our organizations remain structured around a functional model of what a library offers that arose before personal computing and the Internet. We do not consider radical approaches to collections, such as only ever purchasing anything when someone needs it and when it falls below a certain price, leveraging scaled marketplaces like so many online booksellers, and instead look to the same vendors who locked us into unsustainable models for "patron-driven acquisition" approaches that aren't evolving as quickly as our users' attachment to their devices—themselves formerly known as "PDAs" but now a primary lens and companion for information seeking where they are locked into the aforementioned commodity marketplaces where we have no leverage. And we do not seek to create new forms of leverage, such as demanding better licensing terms, reasonable price controls, or systems API parity to simplify delivery. Nor do we attempt to create our own marketplaces, banding together to create a noncommercial e-book platform, the start-up investment for which might be lower than you think, now that we have multiple successful commercial vendors showing us how it can be done.

The twentieth century saw succeeding generations of technology complement, surpass, regulate, and overturn themselves in a fit of public policy arcs that could excite any lawyer, lawmaker, businessman, engineer, or economist. If you study these arcs and shifts, you find common themes such as universal service, common carriers, and balanced priorities among public and private interests that allowed enormous companies to profit without leaving consumers behind in access to commodity information services and technology. It's no secret that in recent years the rate of change of technology has moved so fast that such attempts at setting policies that might balance interests could seem old-fashioned. To consider how the breakup of Ma Bell took nearly a decade but resulted, two decades later, in a resurgent AT&T, or to consider the federally challenged monopoly power Microsoft exerted over its supply chain to lock consumers into its preferred software applications, now themselves nearly irrelevant, is to realize that the very idea of maintaining a consistent balance across interests was old-fashioned decades ago. Either way, we know we have a digital divide along income lines, we know we have dominant technology and information purveyors who succeed wildly in locking down their platforms and ecosystems, and we know we and our libraries are here to serve users who mostly haven't looked to us first for information in over a decade.

This happened under our watch, and we've done little to stop it. The library we know existed for the past century right at the fulcrum of that balance between public and private interests in information and technology marketplaces. Who are we to stop the march of industry toward ever-stricter copyright enforcement, destruction of fair-use and first-sale rights, and unequal, incompatible marketplaces for commodity goods?

We're librarians, and it's our job to fight. If we stay complacent, backed into the corners we've long since huddled into reactively, failing to imagine bold moves we could take to move markets and to support intellectual and commercial freedom, willingly giving over our collections and information safekeeping functions to conglomerates, letting our services suffer, and not fighting for the rights of our community members to make choices about how they seek, manage, maintain, and share information, no one will fight for the library and the balance we long enjoyed but have now lost.

Perhaps our best strategy is to let the library crumble.

I reject flip criticisms in weighty high-culture publications arguing that "libraries must move past books." There have been so many, and their authors understand so little. I see how busy my colleagues are, how steady demand for our services remain, and how stretched we become in keeping up supply. The library has always been a more dynamic, more subtle, and more layered construct than anyone who hasn't spent years moving through them can conceive. But whatever you and I thought we were entering at the start of our careers is a place and time we have already left behind, and to think anything else is to delude ourselves.

Where do we head next? I can only offer a few concrete ideas. Earlier, I mentioned our current generation of administrators and their pre-Internet career foundations; it is a mistake to continue to look for leadership and mentoring from our current leaders. If you wish to lead, and know you need help getting there, look to the leaders you admire most outside of your workplace, and find ways to bring what they have to teach you to how you think about moving yourself and your organization forward. If what the library offers is a rich dynamic—transcending technology, whether that of decades ago, today, or years from now—and if we want to invest in, nurture, and sustain that dynamic, we will only accomplish that with the impact of leadership that transcends the idea of the library we must now discard, and to find that, we must look everywhere.

For our collections, the strategies we use to move them around, and the deals we sign to glue them together, we must know to say "no" to arrangements that place the communities we serve on the wrong side of the increasing imbalance of rights and expenses. If we choose to pay more, we must demand more in exchange or walk away.

Finally, the idea of technological disruption (see Christensen's work for more) holds that entrenched market leaders rarely succeed at defining and deploying truly disruptive innovations; it does not happen inside an organization optimized for doing something else. If those older organizations want to play in the new fields, they have few options: they may acquire new firms outright, or they may spin off nearly independent subsidiaries to compete in new ways. With the former off the table in our cash-strapped not-for-profits, the latter is a possibility, but it would require imagination and determination and true, deep independence. I hope that some of us will choose that path, and that along it, we find the imagination and leadership to steer us ably down it.

Daniel Chudnov is a hacker/librarian and is director of scholarly technology at George Washington University's Gelman Library.

VI

My Turn

Chapter Twenty-Four

Joseph Janes

The library in 2020 will be.

More than likely.

That alone might feel reassuring—2020 is a pretty short timeframe, so it isn't all that daring a prediction, after all. Frankly, I'm less concerned about 2020 than I am with 2025, and 2040, and 2100, and so on. We're not playing a short-term game, at least we shouldn't be, though we also kind of are. There's no long-term strategy without a short-term component, however, so as usual, we're going to have to play multiple, sometimes perhaps competing or contradictory, simultaneous games to be sure of being relevant and vital for today and tomorrow and for lots of tomorrows after that.

There have been libraries, or at least something like libraries, for thousands of years, not quite as far back as recording information goes, but far enough that we're societally used to the idea. First, as always, there's the stuff.[1] Clay tablets, papyrus, scrolls, parchment manuscripts, books, pamphlets, government documents, LPs, slides, what have you. It all begins with the creation of these objects, then they start to accumulate, first in small numbers, then more, then into piles, then into more sophisticated, organized piles, then into something that starts to merit the word "collection." Underlying all of this are important and now (hidden) ideas that saving things can be worthwhile, that putting like things together can be handy, and moreover that having a way to distinguish between them and find one in particular can be even more handy, so structure and metadata and structured metadata start to arise.

As these collections grow in size, complexity, use, and importance, they begin to evolve institutions to maintain them and to attract and even engender people who want to work with them for a living. These institutions and professionals then get more detailed and focused and specialized—and here we are, young-adult-collection-development specialists, Web architects, CJK-serials catalogers, prison-library literacy advocates, and all. It seems hard to imagine there won't be *something* deserving of the name "library" going forward, but what? Especially in a future society where we know that stuff is going to be increasingly digital, co-created, non-textual, and produced outside the traditional publishing context.

It's worth spending just a moment on this shift in publishing and distribution. We've all seen the mergers, acquisitions, and consolidation in many sectors of the publishing industry, loosely defined—trade books, scholarly communication, film studios, recording companies, newspapers, and the like—and the result is fewer and fewer entities controlling more and more venues for distribution and publication of the stuff, at least the stuff we've been used to dealing with. Increasingly, that feels to me like a hand, gradually clenching to hold more things in its grasp more tightly, with the kinds of results we've seen in pricing structures, sales practices, increasingly heinous rights-management regimes, and so on.

The fascinating thing, to me, is the simultaneous development of (so far) free and freely available ways of communicating. If you've got a poem you want to be read, you no longer have to wait for a sympathetic editor at the *New Yorker* or *Poetry* magazine to deign to include you in their canon; you can post it on your blog, and maybe you'll get lucky. Make a YouTube video, and you can be discovered. No doubt this century's Oscar Wilde is developing a following via tweets. In contrast to the closing fist of traditional media, this opening hand seems to be providing the opportunity for developing new forms and genres, including, for example, new modes of scholarly communication. The open-source journal and the scholarly blog are likely the merest beginnings of throat clearings along those lines. What will happen when scholars are able to incorporate, say, live video streams into their work, to give an authentic picture of climate change as manifested in polar-ice-cap melting? Or spreadsheets with their original data to permit new analyses and interpretations or commentary from readers? And as scholarship begins to inhabit those forms and scholars get used to them, those forms will no doubt begin to influence how the scholarship is written and composed and critiqued and conceived; new questions will be asked, new methods of investigation will be developed, and scholarship itself will evolve. It happened in the seventeenth century when the journal arose; it's hard to imagine it won't happen again in the twenty-first. And then, as we know, somebody's got to figure out how to go about evaluating, collecting, organizing, storing, saving, and searching—and all the traditional stuff as well—and making it all work together.

More to the point, and more pointedly, libraries now squarely confront the same question being faced by our colleagues in bookstores, newsstands, record stores, travel agencies . . . : whither the middleman in a peer-to-peer world?

For what it's worth, in the short run, the next few years at least, inertia will continue to be in play. Institutions and professionals will proceed in a more or less familiar (dare one say comfortable?) fashion. That's not intended as criticism; it's normal and to be expected and even valued in any context. Most aspects of libraries as places and collections, as well as services to communities, will persist, with changes minor and occasionally less so, as we've seen over the last several years.

However, there will come a time, sooner or later, when library-as-glorified-study hall/community center/day care/coffee shop won't cut it any longer. Much as I like and appreciate innovations such as food and drink services, gaming, makerspaces, and their cousins, we ultimately have to justify, to our communities and to ourselves, why they belong or are necessary in a library. And as often and as much as I use my university library's research/learning commons, I'm not sure I could give a compelling or convincing reason why it couldn't just as easily be housed in a residence hall, classroom, or student-union building. Not that those arguments can't be made—and not that some of these ideas and services couldn't be more libraryesque—they just haven't yet, at least not universally. It seems likely, soon enough, that these kinds of information-lite innovations will be too thin a broth, and more substance will be required.

We also know that access to technology—hardware, software, and bandwidth—is also a major selling point for libraries today and rightly so. There are still substantial numbers of people and proportions of communities, both public and academic, who have limited technological access or who just prefer another venue for use of technology, so helping to fill those gaps falls naturally as well as squarely in our laps. Over the long haul, though, especially with the proliferation of mobile devices, the need for this sort of access will likely slowly erode.

WHICH WAY ARE THE WINDS BLOWING?

Technology will undoubtedly continue to get faster, both in processing power and bandwidth. It will also get smaller and more mobile and thus ever more personal. Information, or "content" if you will, will continue to get freer (in the opening hand/Google Books mode) and dearer (in the closing fist/traditional media mode), as well as easier to search, find, share, point to, and discover.

If those trends were to continue to their logical end, we'd wind up in a situation where everything would be free,[2] ubiquitous, and able to be perfectly searched for each individual. That's highly unlikely, for all sorts of reasons you're already rehearsing in your mind, but it's hard not to imagine we'll continue to move further down that road as time goes on. More people will have more access to more stuff in more places and more situations. Nothing new there—that describes the last twenty years pretty well—and for the record, that scenario is a win in most aspects and for most people.

It also means that *access*, in the ways we generally traditionally think about it, in the long run, will continually be less the issue at hand. If that's the case, then conceiving of our institutions and professional focus as being primarily about access, and presenting ourselves that way to our clientele, is not a winning strategy because that access will be less and less necessary and desired and thus desirable. Not that it won't be needed—just less so.

Libraries don't have a monopoly on access provision. Nor did we ever; we've always been one of a number of organizations, institutions, vehicles, and mechanisms by which people could become more informed, and there are now way more of those mechanisms than in days gone by. I remember coming across an article, I think from *Library Journal*, describing war information centers set up in public libraries during World War II that would post maps and the latest dispatches; in an environment where newspapers and radio were the most timely and available sources, followed by magazines and newsreels and that's about it, public libraries and those centers filled an important void. It's also likely that those centers provided a valuable community meeting, discussion, and support function as well, as people came together to find out what was going on, talk about it, and hope for the best for their nation and their friends and loved ones in harm's way.

But it's difficult to imagine any such equivalent in today's world. Then as now, there are many neighbors and competitors to libraries, from our colleagues—the archives and museums, publishers, bookstores, and search engines—through to more distant relations, such as zoos, social media, and massively online open courses, all of which exist in at least some part to provide access to information.

WHAT WILL BE (PROBABLY)

So, to my mind, what libraries are going to have to be cannot solely or even primarily be about access because, with the exception of the exotic, the unique, and the prohibitively expensive (local historical materials, shockingly priced scholarly media, the treasures that most of us have locked up somewhere that I hope to heaven you're doing something with and telling your clientele about), access is not the right game to be in now. If you're in the business of passing around somebody else's stuff, you won't be in business for much longer, I fear.

OK, fine. What next, then, smart guy? Here's my 35 cents on what seems most likely to me, going forward:

* *Libraries will continue to be a hybrid of the physical and the virtual, somewhere and everywhere.* A no-brainer.
* *There will be stuff.* Especially books. Why? Because people like books, associate us with books, and likely will for quite a while to come. Having said that, I emphatically do not believe that we completely surrender to a nineteenth-century view of the library, but neither can we or should we ignore that heritage and association—nor, frankly, should we abandon our presence around a form and format with great vigor and potential. We all know that the "book" is undergoing profound transformation, and none of us knows for sure today how that's going to go, or what it will be, do, or look like, but I say we fight for it and maintain our very long-term and hard-won connection to books and what they represent.
* *It will be a product of the past, present, and future.* You could say the same thing about almost any institution from a hospital to a business to a school. The crucial matter, then, is how much and which parts of each and why.
* *It will be made, jointly, in our image, and in the image of what our clienteles want and are willing to pay for.* Let's face it—by necessity, whatever libraries become and do will be a hybrid product of the back-grounds, experiences, prejudices, fears, aspirations, and lessons that librarians will bring to the enterprise. A key component of that is the suite of values that librarians all, well, value and fight for. I include here the ones we all were raised on, such as intellectual freedom, equality of access, protection of intellectual property, conservation and stewardship, and so on, as well as a few I'd suggest adding, such as collaboration, interaction with each other and our communities, creativity, technological sophistication, vision, daring, and risk taking. If we're being honest, our values also, sometimes, include less helpful companions, such as traditionalism, resistance, intransigence, pigheadedness, and an unwillingness to try something (or anything) for fear of failure. In the really short run, some of those latter values work well, particular when you're still skating through inertia, but it won't take much more time before those become suicidal.

On the other hand, let's think about how people generally perceive libraries. Of course, this depends on what you mean and particularly what kind of library. People perceive a cozy neighborhood public library in quite different terms, often, from a grand academic palace. Most people have regular experience with, and exposure to, only a small handful of libraries on a regular basis, so individually, their perceptions are quite localized. Writ large, though, the overall perception of "libraries" thus runs the gamut: from intimate to grand, personal to universal, current and timely to enduring, everyday to noble, community-based to global, selective to comprehensive, modern to timeless. All libraries have aspects of all of these, in various measures and ways. Thus, we are all of these things to them and will so continue to be.

And then—we must already remember that, by and large, we are not them. Yes, we are members of the communities we serve, of course, or certainly should be, but what I mean here is that we are information people. We see the world that way, and based both on inclination as well as training and experience, we can't help it. We know about information, how it works, what can and can't be done, the range of what is and has been, how to find it and use it, and we like it, and we like knowing about it. All of which makes us poorly suited to fully appreciate and understand what it's like to be none of those things: casual or indifferent or ignorant or even hostile to information and libraries, perceiving them merely as means to an end at best, an impediment at worst. Most people don't really grok the information thing, care about it, or even see it as a good or worthwhile thing; consider for a moment what the phrase "information overload" means to most people.

The result of all of this is that we have to meet in the middle, working with people who like us (does anybody really hate librarians?) and respect us but don't fundamentally fully understand what we do or why and how it relates to them. To be sure, dedicated users, friends, people who've had remarkable or personal experiences with libraries and librarians, have different perceptions; I think, though, that this characterization doesn't stray too far from the mark for a large number of regular people.

What they think we are, have been, could be, and should be, combined with what we are, have been, want to be, and are willing to be—somewhere in the midst of that is what we will be.

- *It will be less focused on access and more focused on service.* I think this is a crucial element. We are a service-oriented profession in institutions dedicated to serving clientele and focusing on how we make things better. Articulating how we add value to a highly distributed and often confusing information environment with a lot of crap out there is truly important.

This raises the question of what things we do well, or for that matter, uniquely; what makes us special? Our values, to be sure, and our service orientation, as I've said—I'd add our deep concern and advocacy for literacy in all its meanings and forms, as well as our deep integration into the lives of our communities and clientele, and our concern for the long haul in a world so often focused on the momentary.

A couple of others are worth mentioning in more detail. As I read the submissions for this book, one thing I was trying to pay attention to was what was missing, what nobody talked about. If you've read them (and if you haven't, go back and do!), you know they didn't miss much. On reflection, though, I realize that there's very little here about an area that is dead center of our work and yet so often unrecognized: organization and the intellectual control of information. A shame, though in my defense I did try to solicit a couple of pieces from people in the metadata/organization world, but no dice. In any event, naturally, we know how big a deal that is, both for providing access to materials and resources and also, often for us, for its own sake, to know what we have and don't, what there is and isn't, and perhaps should be. I think we don't always take full advantage of our own metadata in an everyday useful way. Ponder what would happen if you searched for, say, *Romeo and Juliet* in most library catalogs. Likely easier to find a specific edition (or even sometimes a specific item!) for a Shakespeare scholar than any old paperback copy for a teenager, which seems wrong somehow. Yet there is such great power and potential in well-constructed metadata in so many settings.

And then, of course, are our old friends quality, depth, and accuracy and their houseguests detail and authority. It's a $3.95-all-you-can-eat, free/easy/quick/good enough, Googlificated world we're living in, I know, and for most people in most situations, good enough is good enough. That is not our way, though, and for the ones who care, in the situations that matter, going the extra mile, doing the extra search, looking that much more closely at a source, can make a huge difference.

So what's a profession deeply invested in quality and depth to do, faced with a good-enough world? Give in and buy or lease another fifty copies of *Fifty Shades of Grey*? Unlikely, though a little of that here and there doesn't go amiss. It's not a great time to be a middleman these days, as we've seen, but aren't there at least some examples of areas where some sort of similar function or institution is thriving or where quality is appreciated? Sure there is, a bunch I can think of. Competitive sports, arts, performance, all value quality, though that's not altogether helpful. What about, though, the whole organic/sustainable/artisanal world? This seems to be cropping up in lots of venues, from farmers markets and cuisine to design, and while it's on the verge of being overused in a twee sort of way, the desire for things to be handcrafted or authentic or original has some resonance here. Libraries were artisanal back when artisans were . . . artisans. I'd also throw in here customer service of all kinds, including the newly retro "call us and speak to a real person" meme one hears increasingly in credit card and bank commercials. And, of course, the one venue where almost everybody wants high quality all the time is health care. This parallels the information world beautifully, the more crucial the situation, the more is on the line, the greater the need to make sure it's done as well as it can be done. An ATM or a self-serve gas pump will get you reliability and dependability; we can give you way more than that.

AND THUS . . .

Now I get the last word. The library, in 2020, and beyond, will be what it has always been—old and new, familiar and challenging. The fact that the concept of the library, the constellation of ideas that has led people for millennia to collect and store and organize and share information items, is persistent throughout recorded human history tells me that it will endure for the next few years and after that. It's the product of a set of basic, deeply rooted human urges: to communicate, to share and be heard, to learn, to organize, to search, and to make meaning. Where that human activity goes, artifacts are created to record our understandings, our successes and failures, our starts and stops. As that happens, some of us are compelled to go alongside, to gather the products and artifacts of our striving to know and be heard, and to help blaze the trail forward by keeping that stuff safe and making it all work. That work grows ever more valuable by the day, regardless of form or genre or technology.

As I tell my students and anybody else who will listen, librarianship is the most important profession. With us, with the things we do to add value to a chaotic and intensely complicated information world, everything else is easier and better. Our involvement and participation fosters and encourages all kinds of human endeavor, from grand scientific research projects to in-depth family history to looking for the best board book about trucks for a new reader. While there are lots of places and venues where that work gets done, and lots of ways that librarians change lives, the library itself, the institution that combines and represents that work in the mind of so many, retains its centrality and uniqueness. In partnership with those who support us and whom we support, that institution can—if we act with purpose, vision, and courage—thrive as the information environment evolves again and again and again.

NOTES

1. An inelegant word, I know, but I have always liked its earthiness and lack of connotation to any particular format, genre, and so forth. I hope my eighth-grade teacher will forgive me.

2. In a Gresham's law kind of way, free information will tend to drive out dear, absent to some external influence (teachers, importance, etc.).

About the Editor

Joseph Janes is associate professor and chair of the MLIS program at the University of Washington Information School. A frequent speaker in the United States and abroad, he was the founding director of the Internet Public Library and the coauthor of several books on librarianship, technology, and their relationship, including *Introduction to Reference Work in the Digital Age*, and writes the "Internet Librarian" column for *American Libraries* magazine. He is the 2006 recipient of the Isadore Gilbert Mudge award from the American Library Association for distinguished contributions to reference librarianship and served as a member of the ALA Committee on Accreditation. He holds the MLS and PhD from Syracuse University and has taught at the University of Michigan, the University of Toronto, the University of North Carolina at Chapel Hill, the State University of New York at Albany as well as at Syracuse and Washington.